P9-ASN-398

USA TODAY®

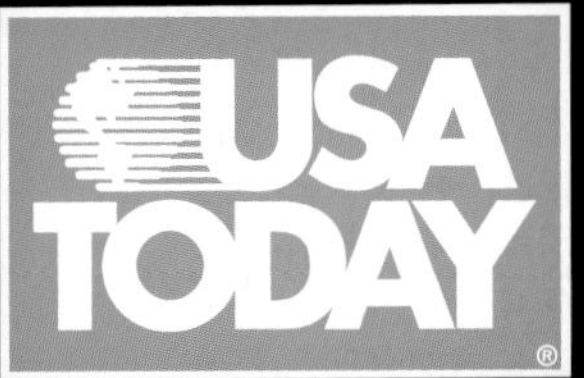

Lifeline

BIOGRAPHIES

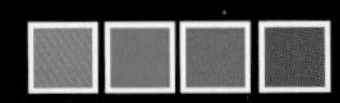

OPRAH WINFREY

Global Media Leader

by Katherine Krohn

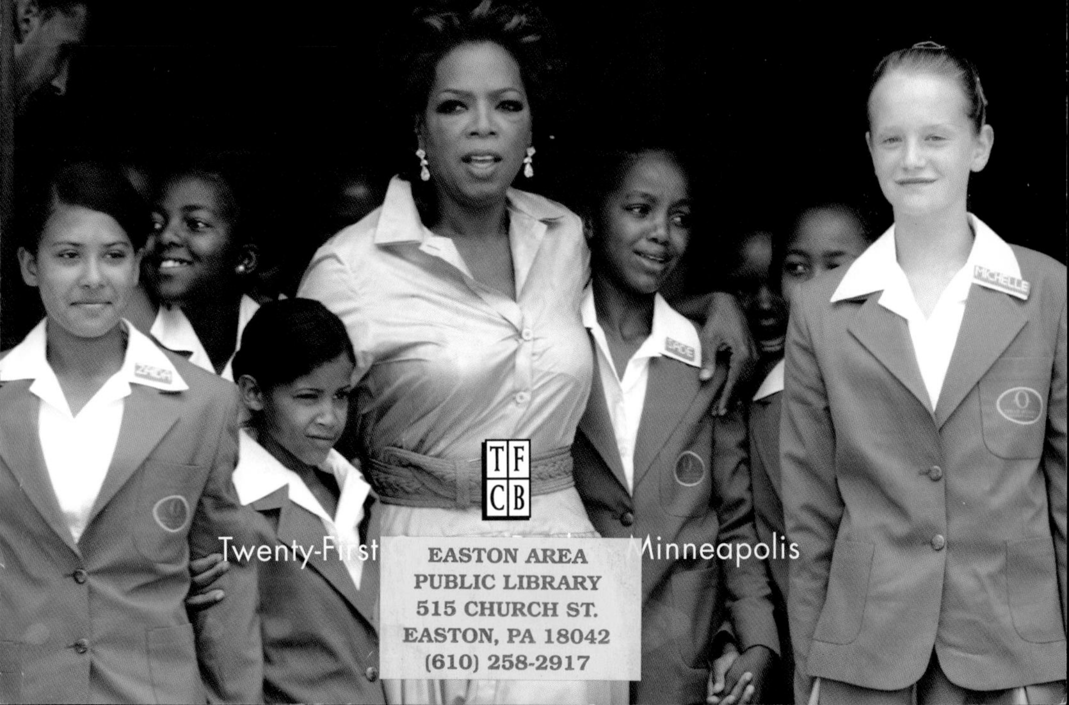

TFCB

Twenty-First … Minneapolis

FOR JACKSON AMOROSE

Twenty-First Century Books
A division of Lerner Publishing Group, Inc.
241 First Avenue North
Minneapolis, MN 55401 U.S.A.

Website address: www.lernerbooks.com

The publisher wishes to thank Richard Curtis, Susan Weiss, and Ben Nussbaum of USA TODAY for their help in preparing this book.

Library of Congress Cataloging-in-Publication Data

Krohn, Katherine E.
Oprah Winfrey : global media leader / by Katherine Krohn.
p. cm. — (Lifeline biographies)
Originally published: Minneapolis : Lerner Publications, 2002.
Includes bibliographical references and index.
ISBN 978-1-58013-571-9 (lib. bdg. : alk. paper)
1. Winfrey, Oprah—Juvenile literature. 2. Television personalities—United States—Bioiography—Juvenile literature. 3. Actors—United States—Biography—Juvenile literature. I. Title.
PN1992.4.W56K76 2009
791.4502'8092—dc22 [B] 2008016951

Manufactured in the United States of America
1 2 3 4 5 6 – PA – 14 13 12 11 10 09

USA TODAY Lifeline BIOGRAPHIES

On the farm: Oprah spent her early childhood on a farm in rural Mississippi, similar to the one shown above.

Farm Girl

Four-year-old Oprah Winfrey stood on the screened-in porch of her grandmother's small farm. She watched her grandmother, Hattie Mae Lee, stir a big black pot of boiling clothes. It was 1958, and Oprah and her grandmother lived in the countryside of Mississippi. Hattie Mae couldn't afford an electric washing machine. Instead, she cleaned her family's dirty clothes in boiling water. "I remember thinking, my life won't be like this," Oprah said later. "It will be better."

Oprah Gail Winfrey was born on January 29, 1954, in Kosciusko, a small town in central

Mississippi. She was born in her grandmother's house with the help of a midwife. Oprah's mother, Vernita Lee, was eighteen and unmarried. She was not in a serious relationship with Oprah's father, Vernon Winfrey. He was a twenty-five-year-old U.S. Army private stationed at Fort Rucker, Alabama.

Vernita's new baby girl was the great-great-granddaughter of Constantine and Violet Winfrey. They were Mississippi slaves who had been freed after the Civil War (1861–1865).

Vernita wasn't sure what to name the new baby at first. A week after the birth, Vernita's sister, Ida, had an idea. She suggested that Vernita name the new member of the family Orpah, after a character in the Bible. But the name was spelled "Oprah" on the baby's birth certificate by mistake. And her name has been Oprah ever since.

During the 1950s, many African Americans in the small towns of the South were very poor. Many black southerners, tired of being poor, moved to northern states in search of work. It was easier to find a job in northern cities such as Detroit, Michigan; Cleveland, Ohio; Milwaukee, Wisconsin; and New York, New York, than it was in the South.

Oprah was only four years old when her mother decided to pack her bags and move to Milwaukee, Wisconsin—without Oprah. Vernita hoped to find work as a maid and make a better life for herself. She planned to send for her daughter once she found a job. Vernita left Oprah with Hattie Mae, Oprah's grandmother. Oprah called her grandmother Mama. Mama was very strict, but she also cared deeply for Oprah.

Chores and Church

Hattie Mae lived on the edge of Kosciusko, and no other children were nearby. Oprah wished she had someone to play with. So she made

Race in the 1950s

When Oprah was a child, it was common for people to be judged by the color of their skin. This racial prejudice was especially prevalent in southern states. For decades, many public schools in the United States were segregated. Black kids went to all-black schools, and white kids went to all-white schools. In 1954, the year Oprah was born, the U.S. Supreme Court made it illegal for public schools to be segregated by race.

Still, other public places in the South remained segregated. Black people were not allowed to use anything marked "whites only," such as drinking fountains and restrooms. Hotels, churches, theaters, and restaurants were segregated. On buses, black riders had to sit in a separate section at the back of the bus. They had to give up their seat if a white person wanted to sit there.

In December 1955, something happened in Montgomery, Alabama, that led to change. An African American woman named Rosa Parks was riding a bus. A white man wanted to sit in her row. Parks refused to give up her seat and was arrested. Her brave action led other African Americans to protest her arrest and the bus segregation laws. Black people in Montgomery refused to ride the buses for 382 days. The bus company lost a lot of money. Because of the protests, the bus company changed its rules so the buses were no longer segregated.

The success of this protest inspired people across the country. They began fighting against segregated businesses in other communities. They fought

friends with the animals on the farm. She gave names to the chickens and pigs and told them stories.

From an early age, Oprah was expected to do chores around the farm. Her grandmother taught her to hang the laundry on the clothesline with wooden clothespins. She also showed Oprah how to make soap from lye, a strong-smelling, powdery white chemical.

so that all Americans could enjoy their civil rights (personal freedoms). The fight became known as the civil rights movement.

Bus protest arrest: Rosa Parks is fingerprinted after her arrest for defying segregation laws in Montgomery, Alabama, on December 1, 1955.

Some of Oprah's tasks were harder than others. Hattie Mae showed her how to kill hogs and chickens. She killed the chickens by wringing their thin necks. "Watch me, 'cause you're going to have to learn how to do this," said Hattie Mae. But Oprah had different plans for her future. "Don't need to watch Grandma," she thought, "because my life isn't going to be like this."

Hattie Mae's house did not have indoor plumbing. Oprah's main chore was to carry water from the well every morning and night. Oprah and her grandmother used the water for drinking, washing dishes, and cleaning themselves with a washcloth. On Saturday nights, Oprah took her weekly tub bath, using water heated on the stove. The next day, she and Mama would be fresh and clean for church.

Oprah's family couldn't afford toys from a store. She had a favorite doll that her grandmother made from a corncob. Although the doll was plain, Oprah thought she was beautiful.

Kosciusko, Mississippi, is named after a Polish patriot, Tadeusz Kosciuszko. He had helped the American colonists during the American Revolution (1775–1783).

Hattie Mae wanted Oprah to grow up reading the Bible. So she taught Oprah to read when she was only three years old. She encouraged Oprah to memorize passages from the Bible and other religious books. Young Oprah had a very good memory. She quickly memorized her Bible verses.

Hattie Mae was proud of her granddaughter and wanted to show her off. She arranged for Oprah to speak at church services at Kosciusko Baptist Church. On Easter Sunday, Oprah stood up to speak in public for the first time. She smiled and spoke confidently in her high-pitched, little-girl voice. "Jesus rose on Easter Day, Hallelujah, Hallelujah . . . all the angels did proclaim." Hattie Mae smiled proudly from her seat in the front row. A woman sitting nearby leaned toward her. "[Hattie Mae], this child is gifted," she whispered, fanning herself with a paper fan.

Oprah's grandmother nodded as the church people praised Oprah's speaking ability. Everyone was impressed that a small child could speak so smoothly and clearly.

Oprah had other chances to recite, when Hattie Mae had company over to the house. "I would just get up in front of her friends and start doing pieces I had memorized," Oprah said. "Everywhere I went, I'd say, 'Do you want to hear me do something?'"

Oprah was encouraged to recite Bible passages. But most other times, she was discouraged from talking in public. Hattie Mae, like many people in her generation, expected children to be "seen and not heard." Children were supposed to stay quiet except when spoken to by an adult.

Oprah's grandmother also believed in the Bible phrase, "Spare the rod and spoil the child." In other words, she felt that children should be punished by being hit. Otherwise, they were likely to grow up spoiled and disrespectful. Oprah was lively and full of spirit. She was beaten almost daily. Oprah's heart sank whenever her grandmother told her to "go get a switch." That meant Oprah was in for another "switching," or beating with a stick. She had to cut a tree branch herself and bring it to her grandmother.

School Days

In the fall of 1959, Oprah started kindergarten in the nearby town of Buffalo, Mississippi. Unlike the other children in her class, five-year-old Oprah could already read and write. She quickly became bored with the simple play and basic lessons of kindergarten.

One day soon after school began, Oprah wrote a note to her teacher, Miss Knew. She wasn't sure how to spell her teacher's name, but she did her best. Oprah's teacher read the carefully printed words: "DEAR MISS NEW. I DO NOT THINK I BELONG HERE."

The teacher was very surprised that Oprah could already write. Right away, she had Oprah moved into the first-grade class. Soon Oprah faced a different kind of move. By 1960 her grandmother had become ill. Oprah was sent to live with her mother in Milwaukee. She left Mississippi and her grandmother forever.

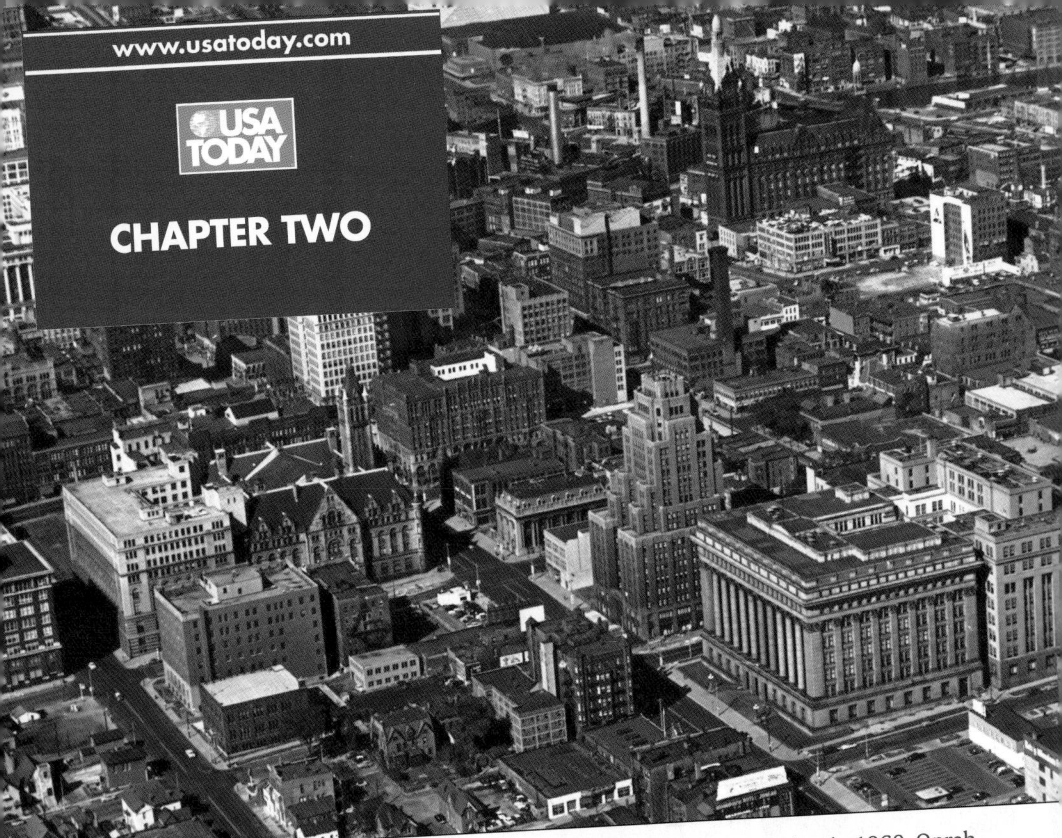

CHAPTER TWO

New city: Oprah moved to Milwaukee, Wisconsin, to live with her mother in 1960. Oprah did not like the bustle, noise, and close quarters of the city.

Where Is My Home?

Oprah's mother grabbed Oprah's book out of her hand. Six-year-old Oprah felt her pulse race and her face get hot. "You're nothing but a bookworm!" her mother yelled. "You think you're better than other kids! Get your butt outside!" Oprah fought back tears and went outside. What was wrong with loving books? she wondered.

Vernita had little education. She didn't understand the beauty and power of books. She discouraged her daughter from reading. And she refused to take Oprah to the public library, the place Oprah most wanted to go.

Oprah didn't like her new home in Milwaukee. It was an industrial city that had many businesses and factories. It was noisy and crowded with people. Everything seemed so strange and different from life on the farm in Kosciusko. Oprah missed her grandmother, her teacher and schoolmates, and the people at church.

Vernita lived in a single room in a boardinghouse on Ninth Street. Her meals were included in the rent. Vernita worked as a maid, cleaning the homes of white people. Her pay was lower than she had hoped to earn. And Vernita had two children to feed. She had recently given birth to her second child, Patricia. Oprah now had a baby half sister.

Vernita worked long, difficult hours. Still, she sometimes had to rely on government welfare money to make ends meet. She had little time to care for Oprah and the new baby. When Vernita did have time at home, she showered the baby with affection, ignoring Oprah.

"[Patricia] was adored because she was light-skinned," Oprah said later. "My half-sister and mother slept inside. I was put out on the porch."

Uprooted Again

The demands of working at her job and raising two children were too much for Oprah's mother. She often left Oprah and Patricia with neighbors in the boardinghouse or with a cousin who lived nearby. Oprah lived with her mother for a little more than a year. In early 1962, Vernita decided that Oprah should go stay with her father in Nashville, Tennessee, for a while. In the meantime, Vernita figured, she would look for a better home for her daughters.

Oprah didn't know her father, Vernon Winfrey, very well. She hadn't seen him since she was a small child. And she had never been to Tennessee. She wasn't sure what to expect.

Vernon had moved to Nashville after his service in the U.S. Army. Nashville was a big, successful city known as the home of the country

Nashville, Tennessee: Oprah moved to Nashville, Tennessee, in 1962 to live with her father and stepmother.

music industry. Vernon had married a woman named Zelma. He had also bought a one-story brick house with white shutters. He worked two jobs as a janitor. One was at a hospital, and the other was at Vanderbilt University in Nashville.

Vernon and Zelma were very happy to have seven-year-old Oprah join their household. They loved kids and were unable to have children of their own. Oprah felt welcome in their home right away. She was thrilled to discover that, for the first time in her life, she would have her own bedroom and bed.

In school Oprah was ahead of most children her age. She was already a strong reader, for example. So her parents allowed her to skip a grade in her new school, Wharton Elementary. Instead of being in second grade, Oprah would be in third. Her father and stepmother wanted Oprah to be prepared for third grade. They spent many hours helping her learn what she needed to strengthen her language and math skills.

Vernon and Zelma were strict parents. They believed that children needed structure in their lives. Vernon and Zelma were not educated themselves, but they understood the importance of schoolwork and reading.

A Reader and Speaker

Oprah's father and stepmother took her to the library soon after she arrived in Nashville. To Oprah's delight, they insisted that she get a library card. "Getting my library card was like citizenship, it was like American citizenship," remembered Oprah.

Oprah liked to daydream. Sometimes she imagined herself as a character in one of the books she was reading. "I read a book in the third grade about Katie John, who hated boys, and she had freckles," said Oprah. "Well, Lord knows, I'm not going to have freckles, no way, no how. But I tried to put some on. And I went through my 'Katie John' phase."

Vernon and Zelma required Oprah to write book reports on the books she checked out of the library. She also had to complete her

Katie John Tucker is the creation of Mary Calhoun. First published in the 1960s, the Katie John series has a loyal following among girl readers. Katie John is a warm-hearted, impulsive tomboy. She gets into many scrapes but still comes out feeling positive and in charge of her life.

regular school assignments. Oprah didn't mind the extra work. She liked to read and study. And she liked the fact that her father and stepmother paid so much attention to her.

Oprah busied herself with schoolwork and was a successful student at Wharton Elementary. She easily moved on to the fourth grade. She especially admired her fourth-grade teacher, Mrs. Mary Duncan. Mrs. Duncan treated Oprah like she was a special person. She gave Oprah attention, advice, and direction.

When Oprah was young, many public schools set aside time during the day for "devotion." This included Bible readings, religious lessons, and prayer. Mrs. Duncan often asked Oprah to lead the daily devotion in class. Some of Oprah's classmates didn't like her, because she was smart and good at reciting.

Each Sunday in church, Oprah would memorize the minister's sermon. Then she recited bits and pieces of the sermon during devotion periods the next week. "My, my, that's just lovely, Miss Oprah Gail," Mrs. Duncan said.

Years later, Oprah's producers surprised her by bringing her favorite teacher, Mrs. Mary Duncan, on her show. Oprah lists it as one of her Top 20 Moments on her show.

Vernon and Zelma were active members of Faith Missionary Baptist Church in Nashville. They were pleased to see how well Oprah could recite Bible passages and stories. Oprah began speaking in church, as she had in Kosciusko.

Once she recited a sermon called "Invictus" by William Ernest Henley. "At the time I was saying it, I didn't know what I was talking about," Oprah recalled. "But I'd do all the motions, 'O-U-T OF THE NIGHT THAT covers me,' and people would say, 'Whew, that child can speak.'"

Vernon and Zelma took Oprah to speak at churches all over Nashville. She became known as the Speaker—the young girl who could speak extremely well. With her talents encouraged and blossoming in Nashville, Oprah felt truly happy for the first time in a long time.

IN FOCUS

"Invictus"

William Henley wrote "Invictus," meaning "unconquered," from his hospital bed in 1875. He suffered from bone disease and had recently had part of his leg amputated. Doctors told him he'd only survive if they amputated the other leg too. Henley rejected this plan and lived.

Out of the night that covers me,
Black as the Pit from pole to pole,
I thank whatever Gods may be
For my unconquerable soul.

In the fell clutch of Circumstance
I have not winced nor cried aloud.
Under the bludgeonings of Chance
My head is bloody, but unbowed.

Beyond this place of wrath and tears
Looms but the Horror of the shade,
And yet the menace of the years
Finds, and shall find me, unafraid.

It matters not how strait the gate,
How charged with punishments the scroll,
I am the master of my fate:
I am the captain of my soul.

www.usatoday.com

USA TODAY

CHAPTER THREE

Not always easy: Growing up, Oprah and Vernita *(shown here in 2005)* did not have an easy relationship.

Back to Milwaukee

When the school year ended in 1963, nine-year-old Oprah traveled back to Milwaukee. It was time for a summer visit with her mother. When Oprah saw her mother again, she was surprised. So much had changed in the past couple of years.

Vernita had moved to a two-bedroom apartment with Patricia. And she had another baby, a boy named Jeffrey. In Milwaukee, Oprah shared a bedroom with her half brother and half sister. She spent the summer reading and looking after Patricia and Jeffrey. She didn't see much of her mother, who worked long hours. When Vernita was home, she spent most of her time caring for her youngest children.

As autumn approached, Vernon arrived in Milwaukee to take Oprah back to Nashville. But Oprah told him she wanted to stay in Milwaukee. She missed her father, her stepmother, and her house in Nashville. But she wanted to please her mother. Disappointed, Vernon returned by himself to Nashville.

Lonely Girl

In Milwaukee, Oprah didn't get nearly as much attention as she had in Nashville. She often turned to television for company. TV was still rather new in the early 1960s. Most U.S. households were just getting television sets.

Oprah's favorite TV shows were about happy families. She loved *Leave It to Beaver*, a funny show about a boy named Beaver Cleaver and his family. She also enjoyed the popular show *I Love Lucy*, featuring comedian Lucille Ball. Oprah thought she might

TV escape: Oprah enjoyed watching the problems faced by Beaver Cleaver *(right)* and his brother, Wally *(left)*, in the *Leave It to Beaver* show.

Funny lady: Comedian Lucille Ball receives a kiss on the cheek from her husband, Desi Arnaz, on the set of their television show, *I Love Lucy.* Lucille Ball's comedy made Oprah think she might want to be an actress.

want to be an actress someday. She might be a famous star like the ones she saw on television and in movies.

Oprah continued to recite sermons and stories in church. She loved to speak—for anyone who would listen. "From the time I was eight years old, I was a champion speaker," she said. "I spoke for every women's group, banquet, church function."

Oprah loved the attention and praise she received when she spoke in public. But privately, she was a lonely child. She deeply wanted love and affection from her mother. But Vernita was usually too busy.

Vernita often left Oprah and her half brother and half sister with a babysitter. One evening in 1963, when Oprah was nine years old, her mother went out. Vernita left the children in the care of their nineteen-year-old male cousin. That night Oprah's cousin raped her. Afterward, she was trembling and shaking and crying. Her cousin took her out for an ice-cream cone. He told her not to tell anyone what he had done.

A couple of years after that attack, Oprah was sexually abused by a family friend and then by an uncle. For several years, Oprah was sexually abused often. "It was just an ongoing, continuous thing," she said. "So much so, that I started to think, you know, 'This is the way life is.'"

When Oprah was a child, most people did not know much about childhood sexual abuse. It was not talked about openly, and no laws existed to protect children. Oprah figured that no one would believe her if she told the truth. She thought she would be blamed for being sexually abused. So, feeling confused and helpless, she kept silent. She tried not to think about the abuse. She concentrated on her schoolwork, on reciting in church, and on reading books for fun.

Oprah had few places to go to get help against child abuse. That's not true anymore. The counselors at Childhelp USA® are available every day. They can be contacted for free by phone at 1-800-422-4453. Their website is http://childhelpusa.org. It has a special section for kids and teens.

In books Oprah could lose herself in other worlds and forget her troubles for a while. When she was a young teenager, Oprah's favorite book was Betty Smith's *A Tree Grows in Brooklyn*. It is the story of

Francie Nolan, a lonely but hopeful poor girl growing up in Brooklyn, New York, in the early 1900s. Oprah stayed up all night long reading the book in the small bedroom that she shared with Patricia and Jeffrey. "There was a tree outside my apartment, and I used to imagine it was the same tree," remembered Oprah. "I felt like my life was like [Francie Nolan's].

In spite of her difficulties at home, Oprah did well in school and earned good grades. But she spent a lot of time alone and had few friends.

Upward Bound

In the mid-1960s, Oprah started attending Lincoln Middle School in downtown Milwaukee. One of the teachers at Lincoln was a man named Gene Abrams. He saw Oprah reading in the school cafeteria every day. Oprah was different from the other students. She wasn't rowdy and loud. She wasn't surrounded by chatty friends like the other girls. Instead, she was quiet and liked to study. She was always reading a book.

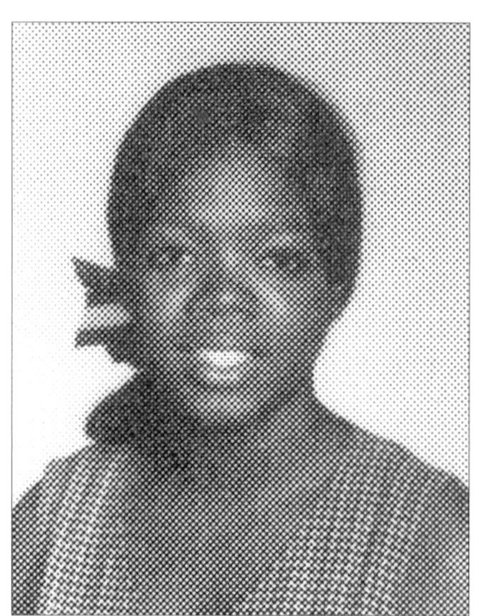

Singled out: One of Oprah's teachers saw her potential and helped her transfer to Nicolet High School. She was the only African American at her new school.

Abrams decided to help Oprah. He helped her transfer to Nicolet High School. Nicolet was an all-white school in the Milwaukee suburb of Glendale. There, Oprah could take part in a program called Upward Bound. Oprah had earned good grades. Through the program, she would have a chance for a better education.

A law, called the Economic Opportunities Act, created Upward Bound in 1964. The program helps bright students from low-income families. The goal is for the students to do well in college entrance tests so they can get into colleges and universities.

Oprah was both excited and nervous about changing schools. Her daily routine changed a lot. She had to ride three buses to get to the suburban school, where she was the only African American student. Oprah still spoke with a southern accent, so she didn't talk like the other kids either. Most of the students at Nicolet were nice to Oprah, and she quickly made friends. But she wasn't sure if people liked her because of who she was or because she was black. "In 1968 it was real hip to know a black person, so I was very popular," Oprah recalled.

It was easy to see the difference between her life and the lives of her white friends. She felt poor. She wished she had nice clothes and a big house like the kids at Nicolet High. Oprah liked her friends, but she couldn't really relate to them. The students at Nicolet had not known many black people—and it showed. "The kids would all bring me back to their houses, . . . bring out their maid from the back and say, 'Oprah, do you know Mabel?'" Oprah remembered.

Troubled Teen

Life at home was also difficult. Oprah still wished for more affection from her mother. Vernita seemed to like Patricia and Jeffrey more than her. Meanwhile, she was still being sexually abused. She had no one to talk to about her experience and feelings. Her unhappiness showed in her behavior. She became wilder during her teen years.

In 1968, when Oprah was fourteen, she was having trouble reading. Her mother took her to an eye doctor. The doctor told Oprah that she needed glasses. Oprah's mother chose the least expensive frames for the eyeglasses. They were old-fashioned frames and shaped like butterflies. Oprah wanted a pair of stylish, attractive glasses. Vernita told her they couldn't afford nicer frames. But Oprah wasn't ready to give up.

She waited until her mother left for work one day. Then Oprah stomped on the new glasses, crushing them to bits. She wanted to make the living room look as if someone had broken in. So she knocked a lamp to the floor and tore down the curtains. Next, she called the police. "We've been robbed," she cried.

When the police arrived at the apartment, Oprah was laid out on the floor. She pretended someone had hit her on the head and knocked her out. The officer was suspicious. He thought Oprah might be faking the robbery.

But when Oprah "came to," the officer took her to the hospital. Workers there called Oprah's mother. Vernita rushed to the hospital in a panic. She, too, wondered if Oprah was acting, but she wasn't sure. In the end, Oprah's trick worked. Her mother bought her a new pair of glasses.

Oprah's behavior grew wilder and wilder. She skipped school, dated many boys, and stole money from her mother's purse. She ran away from home more than once.

One time when Oprah ran away, she headed for downtown Milwaukee. There she saw a big limousine in front of a fancy hotel. Oprah spotted Aretha Franklin, the famous singer, stepping out of the limo. Oprah quickly made a plan. She boldly ran up to Aretha and told her a wild story. She said her parents had kicked her out of the house, and she needed to buy a bus ticket to go stay with relatives in Ohio. Reportedly, Aretha felt sorry for Oprah. She handed her a crisp one-hundred-dollar bill. Oprah happily took the money and stayed in a hotel for a few days. In the hotel room, she lived it up, watching TV and ordering room service.

Oprah's mother didn't understand what had happened to her daughter. Just a few years earlier, Oprah had been a sweet, quiet girl.

Vernita could see that something was wrong, but she didn't know what to do to help. Eventually, her patience wore thin. She looked for another home for Oprah. She called a detention home for troubled teens. But the institution was full. Vernita decided to send Oprah back to her father's house in Nashville. Oprah didn't know if her father would want her either. But she was heading to Nashville anyway.

Teen years: Oprah *(front left)* attended East High School in Nashville from 1968 to 1971.

The Prizewinner

Oprah's father and stepmother had missed her, and they welcomed her back into their cozy house in Nashville. But Vernon and Zelma didn't approve of Oprah's grown-up new look. She wore short miniskirts and heavy makeup. She also had a sassy new attitude. Vernon felt that Oprah's mother hadn't provided her with proper care and direction. He wanted to get Oprah "back on track" in Nashville.

Even with the rules, Oprah was glad to be back in her father's home. Vernon and Zelma's house seemed like a mansion compared to her mother's small apartment. They weren't wealthy, but they had plenty of food and money to buy clothes for Oprah. Vernon now owned his own barbershop.

When Oprah arrived in Nashville, she called her father Pops. Vernon quickly put a stop to that. If she wanted to live in his house, he told her, she would have to follow his rules. She was to call him Father or Dad, not Pops.

Vernon did not know that Oprah had been sexually abused in Milwaukee. Oprah hid another secret from him too. She was pregnant. She was afraid and ashamed to tell him the truth. She hid her pregnancy, wearing baggy clothing until her seventh month. At that point, Oprah's belly was very round. She knew she had to tell her father. On the day she broke the news, she was even more upset than her father was. She was so stressed, in fact, that she went into early labor. She gave birth to the baby that day. The tiny infant died within two weeks.

After her baby died, Oprah felt a mixture of sadness and relief. At the age of fourteen, she didn't feel ready to be a parent. Oprah never said who the baby's father was.

A Fresh Start

In September 1968, Oprah began tenth grade at East High School in Nashville. Because she'd skipped second grade, Oprah was younger than the other tenth graders. She was still adjusting to losing her baby and moving to a new school. At first, her grades were almost all Cs. Vernon pushed Oprah to try harder.

Oprah was often called by her middle name, Gail, throughout high school.

"If you were a child who could only get Cs, then that is all I would expect of you," he told her. "But you are not. So, in this house, Cs are not acceptable."

Oprah tried to see the loss of her baby as a lesson. In a way, she had been given a second chance in life. She was determined to turn her grades and her life around.

Throughout high school, Oprah continued to read a great deal. She especially liked books about women who showed courage in getting through hard times. She read about Anne Frank, the Jewish girl who had kept a diary while her family hid from Hitler's Nazis during World War II (1939–1945). She read about Helen Keller, who lived a full, rich life even though she was blind, deaf, and couldn't talk. Oprah also admired Sojourner Truth. Truth fought for the end of slavery. She also fought for women's rights long before the women's suffrage (right to vote) movement of the early 1900s.

Oprah reads Maya: Maya Angelou *(above, in the 1970s)* and Oprah had very similar childhoods.

When Oprah was sixteen, she read an autobiography that affected her deeply. It was Maya Angelou's 1970 best-seller,

I Know Why the Caged Bird Sings. Like Oprah, Angelou was raised in the South by her grandmother. She later lived with her mother and then her father. She was raped as a child and found comfort in books. "I read it over and over," said Oprah. "I had never before read a book that [described similar life situations]."

Little did Oprah know that Maya Angelou would later become one of her closest friends. Oprah gave Angelou a huge sixty-fifth birthday celebration in 1993. That same year, Angelou dedicated a book of poetry to Oprah.

Vernon and Zelma Winfrey continued to encourage Oprah's studies as well as her talent for public speaking. "We knew she had great potential. We knew she had a gift and talent to act and speak," said Oprah's father. "She's never been a backseat person, in school or in church. She always loved the limelight."

Oprah attended Faith Missionary Baptist Church each Sunday with her father and stepmother. She sometimes gave Bible readings there. She also spoke at other area churches and clubs.

Her talent earned her wider recognition in 1970. That year she won a speech contest sponsored by the Elks Club. Oprah was filled with happiness when she took the prize, a four-year college scholarship. This award for doing well would provide her with money for college. She would begin looking at her college options next year, when she was a senior.

Winning Contests

Besides earning good grades in school, Oprah was also popular. In 1971 Oprah ran for vice president of the student council. Her slogan was "Vote for the Grand Ole Oprah." It was a funny takeoff on the Grand Ole Opry, the famous Nashville concert hall for country music. Oprah was thrilled when she won the election.

Later that year, Oprah and another student were chosen to represent the state of Tennessee at the White House Conference on Youth. They were chosen because of their excellent grades and leadership abilities. The conference was held in Estes Park, Colorado. Oprah met teens from all over the country. When she returned to Nashville, Oprah was interviewed by disc jockey John Heidelberg on WVOL, a local radio station. He talked to her about her experiences at the conference.

A few months later, Heidelberg called Oprah again. He asked her if she'd like to represent the radio station in the Miss Fire Prevention contest. This was a teen beauty pageant in Nashville. Oprah wasn't sure at first. A beauty pageant? She had never thought of herself as a "beauty." But she figured it would be fun to enter anyway.

At the pageant, Oprah paraded before the judges in her new evening gown. She didn't think she stood a chance of winning. No black person had ever won the title of Miss Fire Prevention. And all Oprah's opponents were white girls with "fire" red hair. Because she didn't think she had a chance of taking the crown, Oprah felt relaxed and confident.

One part of the contest was a question-and-answer category. The judges asked each contestant a question. The teen was supposed to come up with a thoughtful, intelligent answer. The first question was "What would you do if you had a million dollars?" One contestant said she would buy a truck for her father. Another teen proudly said that she would buy her brother a motorcycle and her mother a new refrigerator.

Soon it was Oprah's turn to answer the question. She thought a moment. She decided to just have fun with her answer. "If I had a million dollars," Oprah began, "I would be a spendin' fool. I'm not quite sure what I would spend it on, but I would spend, spend, spend." The judges loved Oprah's funny and truthful answer. They asked the contestants a second question: "What do you want to do with your life?"

The other teens all said they wanted to be teachers or nurses. Oprah hadn't really decided what she wanted to be. But she figured she had to say something different from everyone else. That morning she had seen Barbara Walters on TV's *Today Show*. Walters, a broadcast journalist, reported news stories for the show. "I want to be a broadcast journalist because I believe in the truth," Oprah answered. "I'm interested in proclaiming the truth to the world."

Being like Barbara: By her late teens, Oprah had already found a person to emulate. She was broadcaster Barbara Walters *(above)*, who dismantled many barriers for women in journalism.

The judges were impressed with Oprah. She had a winning personality. And with her intelligence, she outshined the other contestants. Oprah was crowned Miss Fire Prevention of 1971. "I know it's not a biggie. But for me it was special," Oprah said. "I was the only black—the first black—to win the darned thing."

The people at radio station WVOL were proud of Oprah. They gave her a watch and a digital clock. Even better, they asked her if she wanted to hear how her voice sounded on tape. Oprah eagerly agreed.

Oprah had had lots of speaking experience over the years. Because of it, she sounded almost like a professional news anchor. The anchor of a news broadcast is the person who reads the news and introduces reports by other reporters. "They couldn't believe how well I read," Oprah said later. "They said, 'Come hear this girl read.' Then someone else listened, and before I knew it, there were four guys standing there listening to me read."

High school graduate: A lot was already happening in Oprah's life by the time she'd reached her senior year. Here she's shown in a picture from her high school yearbook for 1971.

Oprah was only seventeen years old and still in high school. Even so, she was offered a part-time job as a news reader. Oprah was thrilled. After school she hurried to the radio station to do newscasts at three thirty in the afternoon She was doing something she liked, and she was getting paid for it!

College Bound

In June 1971, Oprah graduated from East High School. A few months later, she went to college using her Elks Club scholarship. She attended Tennessee State University, an all-black school in Nashville. She planned to study speech and drama. To save money, she would continue to live with her father and stepmother. She would travel the short distance to school every day. Oprah didn't want to give up her news reader job. So she continued to work part-time at WVOL.

Many issues inspired strong feelings in students. At Oprah's all-black university, many African American students were rallying for "Black Power." Black Power meant trying to get more power for black Americans through political and sometimes violent activism.

Power salute: Black Panthers raise their fists in the Black Power gesture, asserting unity and demanding fundamental changes. Oprah had a hard time relating to the Black Power movement.

"It was a weird time," Oprah said later. "This whole 'black power' movement was going on then, but I just never had any of those angry black feelings. Truth is, I've never felt prevented from doing anything because I was either black or a woman."

Oprah wasn't interested in politics or protesting. She was much more interested in succeeding in school. She wanted to build on her talents and move ahead with her life. That led her classmates to dislike her. They expected black people to be involved in protests during this highly political time. Some students even called her an Oreo. This is an expression for a black person who is considered "white on the inside and black on the outside." Oprah grew to hate college.

IN FOCUS

Going Places

While in Hollywood, Oprah visited the Walk of Fame on Hollywood Boulevard. Hundreds of golden stars, each matched with the name of a famous film or TV star, decorate the sidewalk. Oprah told her father that one day her star would sit beside the others. Oprah's father didn't laugh. He, too, knew in his heart that his daughter was going places.

Father and daughter: Vernon Winfrey *(shown here in the 1980s)* believed in his daughter's intelligence and drive.

In 1972 Oprah entered and won her second beauty pageant, the Miss Black Nashville contest. Then she won a third pageant, Miss Black Tennessee. Oprah was surprised to win these contests. She didn't see herself as beautiful. And she downplayed her calm manner, personality, and talent. "I did not expect to win, nor did anybody else expect me to win," she said. "And Lord, were [the other contestants] upset. I said, 'Beats me, girls, I'm as shocked as you are.'"

Being crowned Miss Black Tennessee landed Oprah a place in the Miss Black America pageant. It was held in Hollywood, California. Oprah didn't win the contest, but the experience inspired her to set her goals high and reach for her dreams.

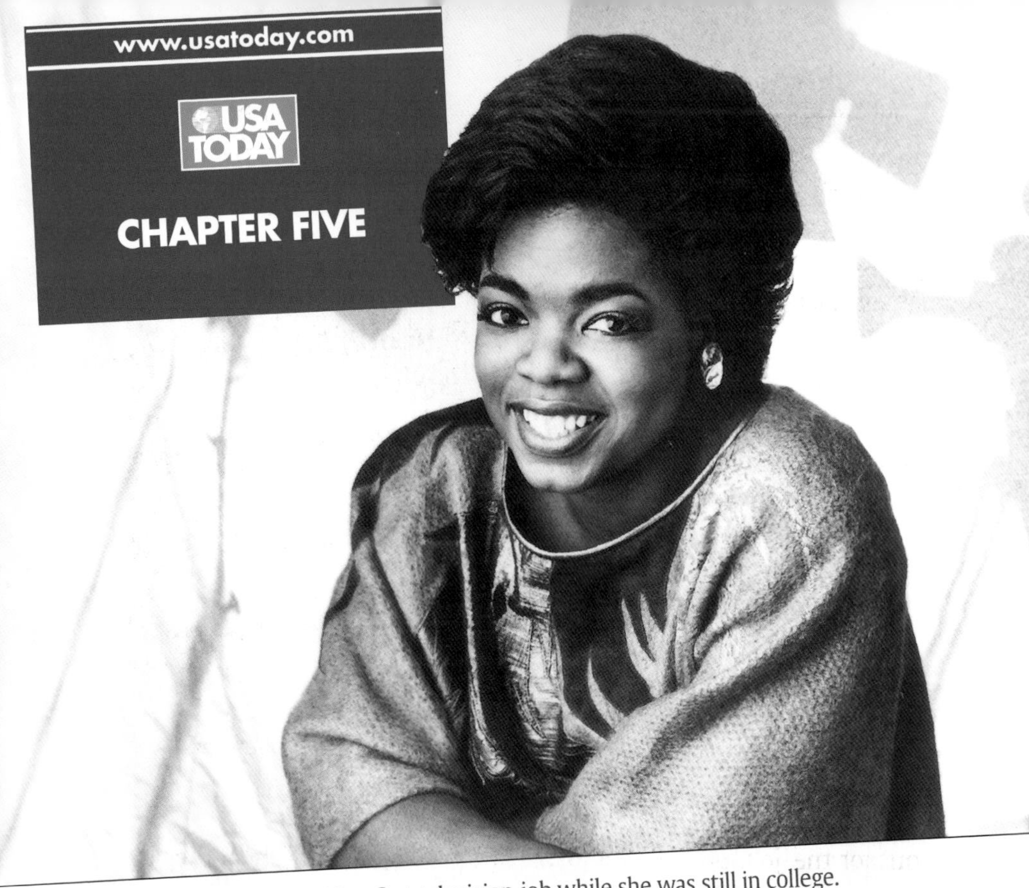

First job: Oprah landed her first television job while she was still in college.

People Are Talking

In college Oprah attended classes, studied hard, and did a lot of reading. In her job as a news reader at radio station WVOL, she gained valuable, real-life experience.

In 1973 Oprah received a phone call from a station manager at WTVF-TV, the CBS television station in Nashville. The manager told Oprah that he had heard her on the radio and was very impressed with her talent. He wanted to hire her to anchor the evening news.

Education: Oprah attended Tennessee State University in Nashville *(above)*, but she found her career before graduating.

Oprah couldn't believe it. They wanted to hire her as an anchor? She was only nineteen years old. Oprah didn't think she could handle both a full-time job and college. She turned down the offer.

The station manager didn't give up easily. He called Oprah two more times. He tried to talk her into trying out for the job. She felt confused. She thought she might rather be an actress than a broadcaster. Oprah asked one of her favorite speech professors at Tennessee State for advice.

He couldn't believe that Oprah didn't take the job right away. "I've seen some stupid people," he said with a laugh. "Don't you know that's why people go to college? So that CBS can call them?" Oprah thought carefully about her teacher's words. She decided to try out for the job. It could be a great opportunity.

At the audition, Oprah wasn't sure how to act. She pretended to be TV journalist Barbara Walters. "I would sit like Barbara, or like I imagined Barbara to sit," Oprah said later. "I'd look down at the script and up to the camera because I thought that's what you do, how you act. You try to have as much eye contact as you can—at least it seemed that way from what I had seen Barbara do."

Oprah landed the job. She was excited about her salary—fifteen thousand dollars a year. It was a lot of money to her at the time, as much as her father was making as a barber. Best of all, she didn't have to quit school. She could go to classes during the day and work in the evening.

At that time, companies in the United States had to follow new affirmative action guidelines set up by the government. Businesses had to ensure that a certain number of the employees they hired were minorities, such as African Americans or Asians. Some critics accused Oprah of being a "token" at the station, just filling the role because she was black. Oprah didn't care if she was the station's token black or not. She was happy with her new job, and she knew she was good at it. She was the first black newscaster in Nashville history. She was also the youngest.

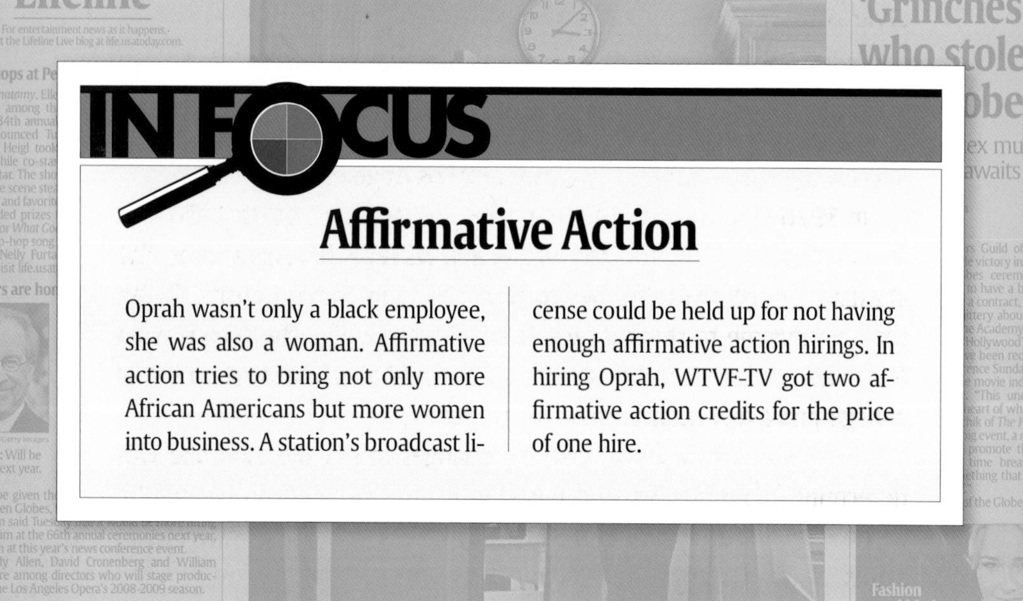

IN FOCUS

Affirmative Action

Oprah wasn't only a black employee, she was also a woman. Affirmative action tries to bring not only more African Americans but more women into business. A station's broadcast license could be held up for not having enough affirmative action hirings. In hiring Oprah, WTVF-TV got two affirmative action credits for the price of one hire.

Learning the Ropes

Oprah's first year as a TV news anchor had its ups and downs. One evening during a live newscast, Oprah made her first big on-the-air mistake. "I was doing a list of foreign countries. . . . And I called Canada 'ca-NAD-a,' recalled Oprah. "I got so tickled. 'That wasn't ca-NAD-a. That was CAN-ada.' And then I started laughing. Well, it became the first real moment I ever had. And the news director later said to me, 'If you do that, then you should just keep going, you shouldn't correct yourself and let people know.' So that was, for me, the beginning of realizing, 'Oh, you can laugh at yourself, and you can make a mistake, and it's not the end of the world.' You don't have to be perfect—the biggest lesson for me for television."

Oprah didn't have to be perfect, but she did want to do her best. She studied tapes of news broadcasts she had done to find ways to improve her news delivery. She worked on her timing, rhythm, and ease in front of the camera. Soon she had developed her own warm, casual style. And she didn't copy Barbara Walters anymore.

After gaining experience at WTVF-TV, Oprah knew she wanted to continue her career in television broadcasting. She began to look around for a better broadcasting job. She sent tapes of herself to stations in big cities such as New York and Los Angeles.

In 1976 Oprah received a tempting job offer. It was at WJZ-TV in Baltimore, Maryland. The job was as a news reporter and anchor. The station managers wanted her to start soon—in three months. Oprah took some time to think it over. If she left Nashville, she'd be leaving her father and stepmother's home. She would also have to drop out of college just a few months short of graduating.

But Oprah was used to fast, big changes in her life. And she was determined to move forward with her career. The new job would be an upward move. It would mean a pay increase and a position at an important television station. Oprah decided to accept the job.

Hello, Baltimore

Twenty-two-year-old Oprah arrived in Baltimore in June 1976. She couldn't wait to start her new job. Meanwhile, she rented her first apartment, shopped for new work clothes, and explored the large, bustling city of Baltimore.

WJZ-TV placed billboards all around Baltimore to advertise Oprah's upcoming first appearance at the station. The billboards read: "WHAT'S AN OPRAH?" Oprah didn't like the billboards much.

On August 16, 1976, Oprah made her first appearance on the six o'clock news at WJZ-TV. For the show, she wore a bright red suit. Her hair was styled in an Afro, a popular hairstyle at the time. Unlike many young people who are starting a new job, Oprah was calm and confident. Her years of public speaking and her anchoring experience made her comfortable in front of the cameras.

Baltimore, Maryland: Oprah moved to Baltimore in 1976 to work at WJZ-TV *(above, as it looked in 2007).*

Oprah read the news in a warm and friendly style. She came across as a real, down-to-earth person. But to some people, she was a little too real for the evening news. Sometimes she changed the words of the stories that she read. She wanted to make the news stories sound more casual. And she often showed personal feelings about the stories she reported.

"My openness is the reason I did not do so well as a news reporter," Oprah said. "I used to go on assignment and be so open that I would say to people at fires—and they'd lost their children—'That's okay. You don't have to talk to me.'" Oprah's news director wasn't as understanding. He said, "What do you mean they didn't have to talk to you?" Oprah replied, "But she just lost her child, and you know I just felt so bad."

For one assignment, Oprah was sent to report on a funeral. But she refused to go into the funeral home. She felt sorry for the families involved, and she didn't want to disturb anyone. Sometimes when Oprah was reading an especially sad story, she would even cry on the air. Oprah's bosses didn't appreciate her natural and open style of reporting the news. In Nashville, audiences had liked her easygoing, friendly manner. But the people of Baltimore expected a more polished news anchor. Oprah didn't have the slick appearance of the other news anchors in town.

Clouds and Silver Linings

Oprah had signed a two-year contract with the station, so the managers couldn't fire her. Instead, they took her off the evening news and gave her a five-minute time slot at five thirty in the morning. The bosses said she had been moved because she was so good that she needed her own time slot. But Oprah knew better. She had been given a less important job.

"I was [deeply hurt] because up until that point, I had sort of cruised," she said. "I really hadn't thought a lot about my life, or the direction it was taking. I just happened into television, happened into radio. . . . I was twenty-two and embarrassed by the whole thing because I had never failed before."

Meanwhile, the station managers decided that Oprah needed a change in her appearance. They sent her to an expensive salon in New York to have her hair straightened and styled. Oprah wondered about their reasons for the decision. Did her bosses want her to look more like the white newscasters?

Going to the salon did not work out well. The hair stylist left the harsh straightening chemicals on for too long. They damaged Oprah's hair so badly that it fell out. She was bald for weeks and had to wear wigs.

Oprah has a round head. When she was bald, it was difficult to find a wig big enough. This fact only brought down her self-esteem even more.

Things didn't get better. The bosses at WJZ-TV didn't like Oprah's speaking voice, either. They had her take lessons from a professional voice coach. Oprah became depressed. Her job didn't feel right at all. But she figured she had no choice but to change the way she talked and looked. She thought it was the only way to keep her job.

She dragged herself to the voice coach's office. But, to her surprise, the coach didn't think there was anything wrong with her voice. She shouldn't let anyone try to change her into someone she wasn't. The coach warned that Oprah would never make it in broadcasting if she didn't stand up to her bosses. But Oprah wasn't even sure she wanted to make it in broadcasting. In her heart, she still dreamed of being an actress.

"I really don't want to do this. What I want to do is act," Oprah told the voice coach. "What I think is going to happen is that I will be discovered because I want it so badly. Somebody is going to have to discover me."

"You are a dreamer," said the coach. Oprah didn't care if she was a dreamer. She headed back to WJZ-TV with a new attitude. She would just ride this out. She would take the morning news spot and wait until something better came along.

Oprah's professional life in Baltimore was rocky, but in her personal life, she made a new friend. Gayle King was another WJZ-TV newscaster. One evening, a sudden snowstorm kept Gayle from going home. Oprah invited her to stay over at her apartment, near the studio. The two bonded instantly. They delighted in the discovery that they wore the same dress and shoe size. They even had the same contact lens prescription. They quickly became best friends.

Best friends: Oprah found a lifelong friend in Gayle King *(right)*. This is a promotional picture for the show *Just Between Friends* that they later hosted together.

Oprah's work life began to improve in 1978, when a new station manager was hired at WJZ-TV. He wanted Oprah to cohost a new morning talk show called *People Are Talking*. Oprah and her cohost, Richard Sher, would be interviewing famous people and some lesser-known people. The show would feature lighthearted, fun interviews as well as serious, personal stories. The new show was a perfect fit for Oprah. "The day I did that talk show, I felt like I'd come home," she said.

She recalled, "My very first interview was the Carvel Ice Cream Man, and Benny from *All My Children*—I'll never forget it. I came off the air, thinking, 'This is what I should have been doing.' Because it was . . . like breathing to me. Like breathing."

IN FOCUS

The Legacy of Phil Donahue

In 1967 Phil Donahue started a talk show in Dayton, Ohio, for what he called, "women who think." Up to that time, most daytime talk shows focused on narrow women's issues, such as housekeeping and cooking. Donahue found that women were passionately interested in the events and issues of the day.

Donahue not only broadened the range of topics. He also taped his show in front of a live audience and encouraged people at home and in the studio to comment on what his guests were saying. He had a knack for asking tough, probing questions in a way that made people want to answer him. Nor did Donahue shy away from controversial topics, such as abortion or homosexuality, that many daytime hosts wouldn't touch.

In 1974 the show moved from Ohio to Chicago, Illinois, and became a national sensation. From 1985 to 1996, it aired from New York. During his more than twenty years as a daytime host, Donahue won multiple Emmy Awards. And later talk show

On *People Are Talking*, Oprah could be herself—warm, friendly, and funny. And viewers liked it. She loved talking with her guests about issues and feelings. And she instantly clicked with her cohost, Richard Sher. He had been a talk show host before.

At first, the management at WJZ-TV was nervous about the new show. *People Are Talking* would air during the same time slot as *Donahue*, hosted by Phil Donahue, a popular talk show host whose show was on all over the country. But within weeks, the bosses relaxed. *People Are Talking* had a larger Baltimore audience than Donahue's show. Women viewers, especially, loved Oprah.

hosts, including Oprah Winfrey, have paid tribute to his pioneering style. As Oprah put it, "If there hadn't been a Phil, there wouldn't have been a me."

Talk show revolutionary: Phil Donahue conducts an interview on his show in the 1970s.

CHAPTER SIX

A new show: Oprah shows her enthusiasm at a taping of *The Oprah Winfrey Show* during its first year.

The Oprah Winfrey Show

Oprah cohosted the top-rated Baltimore talk show for six years. In the fall of 1984, when she was thirty, another big opportunity came her way. A coworker at WJZ-TV told her about a job opening at WLS-TV in Chicago, Illinois. The job was hosting a talk show called *A.M. Chicago*. If Oprah landed the job, she would get a huge pay increase.

On Labor Day, Oprah flew to Chicago, one of the country's largest cities. She recorded a one-hour audition tape. She spoke about herself and a variety of topics. The station manager, Dennis Swanson, watched her audition tape in his office. Swanson walked over to Oprah and pretended to measure her head. "What are you doing?" she asked.

"Your head fits very nicely on your shoulders," said Swanson. "I just want to make sure that when this great success befalls you that it [your head] will always stay there."

"Do you really think I could be that successful?" said Oprah, realizing that she had the job. "Yes, I do," Swanson replied. He added that the station would be in contact with her soon to make a contract for her new position at *A.M. Chicago*.

Top-Rated Talker

Chicago was the home base for Phil Donahue, Oprah's talk show rival. Could she keep up the top ratings she had scored in Baltimore? Donahue had been the first to run the type of talk show that he and Oprah did. The host takes a microphone into the audience and

IN FOCUS

Getting Personal

In contrast to Phil Donahue, Oprah asked personal questions that she thought everyday people would be interested in. Here's an example. Phil Donahue once interviewed the late Dudley Moore, a very short actor who had often dated very tall women. He asked Moore about the details of his upcoming movies. Oprah also interviewed Moore. But she asked Moore how the short-tall dating combination worked!

allows people to make comments or ask questions of the show's guests. Donahue had a simple style and talked mostly about issues instead of feelings.

Oprah, on the other hand, got personal on her show. She shared her own feelings, secrets, and confidence problems with her viewers. On a show about weight loss, Oprah talked about her own struggle with food. Oprah connected with her guests and her audience. When a guest was upset, Oprah usually gave her a hug or touched her hand. She was a different kind of talk show host.

Local show: Relaxed at being herself, Oprah tries on a pair of boots during her show in Chicago in 1985.

Because Oprah shared her feelings, guests were inspired to talk openly about their problems too. "My ability to get people to open up is [because] there is a common bond in the human spirit," Oprah said. "We all want the same things. And I know that."

Oprah loved her job. She didn't think things could get any better—but they did. In 1985, a year after she moved from Baltimore to Chicago, her show got a new name—*The Oprah Winfrey Show*. And the program soon topped *Donahue* in the

Nielsen ratings, which measure a show's popularity. Still, Oprah felt as if something was missing in her life. She had always wanted to act in a film, not just be a TV host.

Set up by Arthur Nielsen, the Nielsen television ratings measure how many viewers watch a particular television show. Rates for TV advertising are based on the ratings. High Nielsen ratings result in high advertising costs.

The Color Purple

One day in 1985, a film producer and musician named Quincy Jones was in Chicago. He turned on the TV and spotted Oprah hosting her hit talk show. He knew right away that she was right for the part of Sofia in the movie he was currently producing. The movie was *The Color Purple.* Oprah had read the book earlier and had loved it.

Great timing: Quincy Jones *(left)* saw Oprah's show in 1985 and knew she would be great as Sofia in *The Color Purple.*

Jones didn't waste time. He contacted the

IN FOCUS

Discovering *The Color Purple*

When Oprah was still in Baltimore, she was flipping through the pages of the *New York Times* Book Review. The paper had an article about a new book by an African American author named Alice Walker. The book, *The Color Purple*, was about Celie, a "poor, barely literate Southern black woman who struggles to escape the brutality... of her treatment by men," the review said.

The book sounded very interesting to Oprah. After reading the review, she went out and bought the book. In fact, she bought every copy of *The Color Purple* in stock. She wanted to share it with friends.

Oprah related to Celie on a deep level because "you know that you are not the only one. Because all of this time, you have carried this burden [of abuse]. You think nobody else in the world has been through this. Nobody else is as bad as you. And then you discover that you are not so bad after all. It's an amazing thing."

Extraordinary author: Alice Walker wrote *The Color Purple.*

film's director, Steven Spielberg. They called Oprah and offered her the role. Oprah had been "discovered," just as she had dreamed of being for so long. She called it "absolutely divine intervention." In the film, Sofia fights back against an abusive husband named Harpo. Harpo was played by Willard Pugh. *The Color Purple* was released in December 1985. Some reviewers liked it, but many did not. Oprah's performance, however, was praised. *Newsweek* magazine called her portrayal of Sofia a "delight."

Some African American men said that *The Color Purple* stereotyped them as always being abusive to women. They protested the movie. Some male reviewers gave it bad reviews.

In 1986 Oprah was nominated for an Academy Award for her performance in the film. Oprah arrived at the Oscars dressed in a beautiful, bead-trimmed, gold and ivory gown. She wore dangling diamond earrings. She also wore a ten-thousand-dollar fox fur coat, dyed bright purple after the movie's title. Oprah looked stunning, but she felt fat. Parts of her dress were so tight she could hardly breathe during the ceremony.

Oscar events: Oprah poses with a life-size Oscar statuette backstage at the Oscars in 1986. She was nominated for *The Color Purple.*

Throughout her career, Oprah had often found comfort in food. She turned to food when she felt stressed. As a result, she had steadily put on weight. At the 1986 Academy Awards, she was almost at her heaviest point.

Oprah did not win an Oscar. Afterward, she tried to make light of her disappointment as well as her weight problems. "Perhaps God was saying to me, 'Oprah, you are not winning because your dress is too tight for you to make it up all those steps to receive the statuette,'" she told a writer for *McCall's* magazine.

Oprah tried not to be too discouraged about her loss at the Academy Awards. She knew that being nominated for an Oscar was a great honor in itself. She also knew that she wanted to continue acting in films.

Meanwhile, *The Oprah Winfrey Show* continued to receive top ratings. In 1986 Oprah signed a deal with King World Productions, Inc.

On a roll: In 1986 Oprah's show started to be aired across the country. She became well known and was recognized across the United States.

King World bought the national syndication rights, so they could broadcast the show to audiences all over the country. People across the United States got to know Oprah, the first African American host of a national TV talk show.

Oprah's fame soon grew enormous. In the late 1980s, she was on her way to give a speech. Her best friend, Gayle, rode in the car with her. They pulled closer to the auditorium where Oprah was to speak. The two friends could see police cars, long lines, and a big crowd of people. A traffic jam clogged the street.

"Who's coming?" asked Gayle.

"I am," said Oprah.

"No, no, I mean, who is really coming? Besides you? Who are all of these policemen for?"

"Me," said Oprah, laughing.

Gayle was shocked. "Oh, my goodness," she said. "What is becoming of you?"

Harpo Productions

Another good thing about national syndication was that Oprah was making a lot more money—nearly $125 million a year. With her increased income, Oprah decided to form her own production company. She called her company Harpo Productions, Inc. Oprah became one of the

By Darryl Haralson and Marcy E. Mullins, USA TODAY, 2002

first women in history to own a TV and film production company. Through her new company, Oprah began to buy the film rights to novels and other literary works, including *Their Eyes Were Watching God* by Zora Neale Hurston and *The Wedding* by Dorothy West. These rights allowed Harpo to make movies based on those works.

Oprah continued to work hard on her talk show. She did shows about child abuse, divorce, being overweight, and many other topics. Whatever the topic, she worked to let people know that they had the power to change their lives. Oprah also stressed the importance of dealing with the past and healing emotional pain. "If you don't heal your personal wounds, they continue to bleed," she said.

Willpower: Oprah struggled with her weight throughout the 1980s—and she wasn't afraid to talk about it on her show. Here she pretends to block access to her refigerator.

In the late 1980s, *The Oprah Winfrey Show* began to change. It focused more on personal and spiritual growth. Oprah hosted guests such as inspirational speaker Marianne Williamson. Williamson encouraged people to reach for their best selves.

Oprah agreed with Williamson's ideas. "As a kid . . . I always wanted to be a minister and preach," said Oprah. "And I think, in many ways, that I have been able to fulfill all of that. I feel that my show is a ministry."

But Oprah isn't just a speaker. "She does something that most people don't have a clue about," said Quincy Jones. "She knows how to listen. And she listens not just with her head. She listens with her heart and soul."

In 1987 Oprah accepted her first Daytime Emmy Award, for Outstanding Talk Show Host. Emmys are awarded every year to recognize the year's best work in television. Oprah's show also won Emmys for Best Talk Show and Best Talk Show Director.

Outstanding: Oprah holds up her 1987 Emmy for Outstanding Talk Show Host.

Love in the Air

Oprah's TV and film career was going great. But her personal life lacked romance. That changed in 1987. She met a man who would stay by her side for years to come.

Stedman Graham was good looking and tall. He was a former model and basketball player. He worked as the executive director of a nonprofit program called Athletes against Drugs. He had been married once and had a young daughter, Wendy. Oprah had met Stedman at fund-raisers and parties around Chicago. But she had never spent time with him.

New friend: Oprah with boyfriend Stedman Graham in 1987

One day, Stedman called Oprah and asked her for a date. Oprah thought he seemed nice, and she liked him. But she was afraid that Stedman liked her just because she was famous and wealthy. So she turned him down. Stedman was determined, however. He called Oprah several times, each time asking her for a date. Finally, she gave in and went out with him. Within weeks, their dating turned into a serious, committed relationship.

Oprah took an important step in her career in 1988. Harpo Productions bought the rights to *The Oprah Winfrey Show*. Oprah had the power to produce her own show, her own way. She planned to start pretaping shows instead of doing live ones. That would give her more flexibility and free time in her schedule. She also wanted to find a new studio for the show and nicer, more comfortable surroundings for her staff.

She was thinking big. She spent $10 million on an 88,000-square-foot production studio. It was west of downtown Chicago and as long as a city block. She then laid down another $10 million to remodel the building. She added a TV studio, staff gym, and fancy offices. She added a movie screening room complete with a popcorn machine. She named the new studio Harpo Studios.

Oprah's empire—the companies she owned and controlled—continued to grow. In 1989 she opened a restaurant with Richard Melman, who had run many restaurants in Chicago. The unusual restaurant was called the Eccentric. It featured the food and look of four different countries—the United States, Great Britain, France, and Italy. The U.S. menu included some of Oprah's favorite dishes. One dish was Oprah's

Eclectic restaurant: Oprah talks to the waitstaff at her new restaurant, the Eccentric, in 1989.

August 4, 1988

Oprah gains more than money in new contract

From the Pages of USA TODAY

When Oprah Winfrey took a morning jog in Chicago on Wednesday, she kept hearing people say, "Hey, Oprah! Give me some money!"

She laughed about it later in a phone interview, but she insists reports of her impending wealth are greatly exaggerated. "It puts me in a terrible position. Let me tell you, (speculative reports of) $100 million is ridiculous. If it's that much, I haven't seen it."

Earlier this week, King World—which distributes her top-rated *Oprah Winfrey Show* to 198 markets—renewed the show for five years, including a deal with ABC's seven owned-and-operated stations. One of them, Chicago's WLS, has produced and been the show's home base for four years.

Potatoes, made with potatoes, horseradish, parsley, and cream. (The restaurant closed in 1995.)

Oprah's power and fame became greater and greater. As it did, the media seemed to bully her more and more. Oprah and Stedman were very happy together, but the media wouldn't leave them alone. "Why aren't you married?" reporters repeatedly asked. The media wrote mean-spirited stories suggesting that Stedman only stayed with Oprah for her money. Tabloid newspapers, such as the *National Enquirer*, were the meanest.

Wednesday, Winfrey's production company—HARPO, Inc. (Oprah spelled backward)—announced it will take over the show's ownership and production duties from WLS, starting this fall.

She says the deals represent "a considerable amount of money," but won't elaborate. "It was time for the transition," Winfrey says. "It puts me in the position to be in control of my time and my life." She plans to hire two producers to join the five already on staff, plus other personnel.

Winfrey says "the show is the thing," and it will continue in rented space at WLS. Eventually, she hopes to get her own Chicago studio.

Winfrey wants to devise a new production schedule, however, to give her more time off. "The whole point is to make it easier. Right now I have four weeks vacation and I took my entire break this year to do (the ABC movie) *The Women of Brewster Place*."

A new schedule might let her add a sixth taped show to her five weekly live broadcasts, creating a backlog that could give her more time off.

Even if the public might start considering her less of a talk-show host than a media mogul, Winfrey says, "It's all sobering and humbling. That's what I wrote in my journal . . . after the very last meeting of the King World lawyers and the ABC lawyers and my lawyer. I won't change in terms of getting too big for my britches. All of this—the dollars, the attention and the so-called fame—doesn't mean anything unless you have the work to back it up."

—Matt Roush, August 4, 1988

Sometimes the press made rude comments about Oprah's weight. She was deeply upset by the articles. "The tabloids used to make me cry all the time," she said. "Every time they would come out with the least little thing about me, I used to [cry]."

Weight Issues

The stories were all the more painful because Oprah badly wanted to lose weight. In 1988, during the summer break from her show, she went on a strict liquid diet. For three and a half months, she ate nothing but a particular diet drink. Because the diet was so extreme, a doctor carefully watched her progress. Oprah also started working out at a gym and jogging. She had lost sixty-seven pounds by the time the fall television season began.

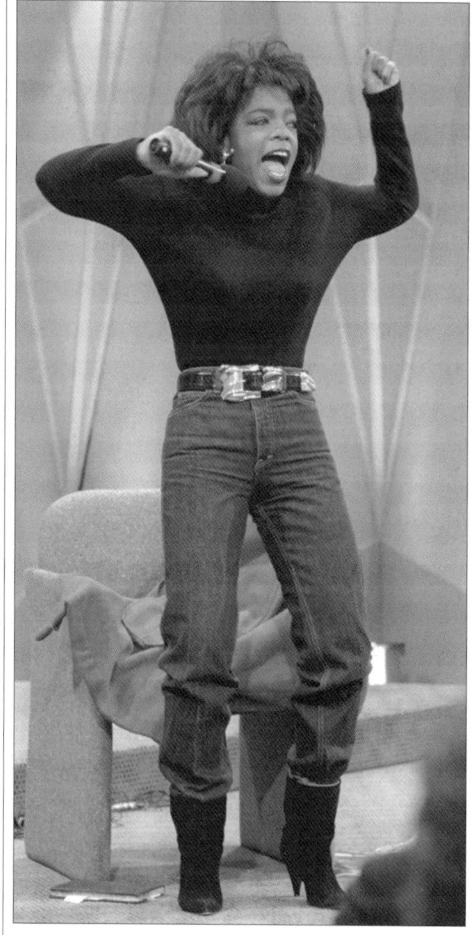

Big change: Big changes in her diet and a daily exercise routine helped Oprah lose sixty-seven pounds in 1988.

On November 15, 1988, Oprah shared her weight-loss victory with her viewers. She came onstage dressed in tight-fitting, size 10 designer jeans. She pulled a wagon filled with sixty-seven pounds of animal fat. The animal fat represented the weight she had lost. The audience clapped and cheered Oprah's success.

Other viewers were not as happy about her newly thin figure. Many people admired Oprah Winfrey because she could be so successful without being thin. What message was she sending now about body image? Some viewers felt that Oprah had let them down.

But Oprah wasn't happy being overweight. She wanted to lose weight for herself more than for anyone else. She felt healthier and more sure of herself. Unfortunately, Oprah gained the weight back quickly. This is

Awards galore: One of the many awards that Oprah won in 1988 was the People's Choice Award for Favorite Talk Show Host.

common for people who follow rapid weight-loss programs.

Oprah's ups and downs on the scale did not slow her career success. Her show continued to pick up top ratings and several awards. Still, the tabloid press continued to give her a hard time. It had been three years since Oprah and Stedman got together. Rumors got started that Stedman was gay.

"That was the most difficult time for me," said Oprah. "I believe in my heart that had I not been an overweight woman, that rumor would never have occurred. If I were lean and pretty, nobody would ever say that. What people were really saying is why would a straight, good-looking guy be with her?"

"He was so brave," Oprah added. "And I never loved him more. He taught me so much during that period. When I handed [the article] to him, he looked at it and said, 'This is not my life. I don't have anything to do with this.'"

Oprah was learning the huge challenges of being famous. She couldn't walk alone with Stedman at a park, for example, without photographers following them. In 1989 Oprah bought a 160-acre farm in Rolling Prairie, Indiana. The farm was a place to get away from the pressure of being famous. The property included an eight-room guesthouse. It also had a charming log cabin, a gym, a pool, and a barn with nine horses.

"I've never loved a place the way I love my farm," Oprah told a writer for *Essence* magazine. "I grew up in the country, which is probably why I'm so attached to the land. . . . I love the lay of the land. I love walking the land. And I love knowing that it's my land."

Oprah liked spending time on her farm because she could unwind there and be herself. She didn't have to be "on"—smiling for the cameras. Underneath her stardom, she was a regular person, with problems like anyone else. In 1989 her brother Jeffrey died of AIDS. Oprah had not been in close contact with Jeffrey or other members of her family over the years. Still, his death hit her hard.

Palatial farm: Oprah bought her farm in Indiana in 1989. It has become a peaceful retreat for her and her friends.

Oprah hasn't talked publicly much about her family members or her relationship with them. Oprah says her grandmother, Hattie Mae Lee, who died in 1963, shaped her life the most of all her relatives. "My grandmother gave me the foundation for success that I was allowed to continue to build upon," Oprah said. "My grandmother taught me to read, and that opened the door to all kinds of possibilities for me."

USA TODAY

CHAPTER SEVEN

Protecting children: President Bill Clinton *(sitting at center)* signs the National Child Protection Act into law in 1993 as Oprah *(third from left)* looks on.

New Directions

In 1990 one episode of *The Oprah Winfrey Show* changed the way she looked at herself. She was interviewing a woman who had been severely abused as a child. Because of her abuse, the woman had serious mental health problems. While listening to the woman's story, Oprah thought, "'Oh, that's why I was that way.' I always blamed myself. Even though . . . I would speak to people and say, 'Oh, the child's never to blame. You're never responsible for the molestation in your life.' I still believed I was responsible somehow. That I was a bad girl.

"So it happened on the air, as so many things happen for me. It happened on the air in the middle of someone else's experience, and I thought I was going to have a breakdown on television. And I said, 'Stop! Stop! You've got to stop rolling cameras!' And they didn't, so I got myself through it, but it was really quite [upsetting] for me.

"And I realize that I was the kind of child who was always searching for love and affection and attention, and somebody to . . . look at me and say, 'Yes, you are worthy.' Unfortunately, there are adults who will take advantage of that and misread your intentions."

The show was a turning point for Oprah. From then on, she tried to overcome her need to be a people pleaser. She worked to change her old pattern of wanting everyone to like her. She was determined not to let her childhood abuse keep hurting her.

Oprah realized that she could use her painful past in a positive way. She could help other victims of abuse. "A part of my mission in life now is to encourage every other child who has been abused to tell. You tell, and if they don't believe you, you keep telling," Oprah said. "You tell everybody until somebody listens to you."

In 1991 Oprah told the nation's lawmakers about her abuse. She spoke before the U.S. Senate Judiciary Committee in Washington, D.C. She worked to get a new law passed, the National Child Protection Act. The act established a nationwide database of convicted child abusers.

In 1993 President Bill Clinton signed into law the National Child Protection Act. It was more popularly known as Oprah's Bill.

Taking Control

In June 1992, Oprah accepted her third Daytime Emmy Award for Outstanding Talk Show Host. But she wasn't happy. She said she was embarrassed at having to "waddle my way up to the stage with the nation watching my huge behind." Oprah's weight had climbed to an all-time high of 237 pounds. "I felt like such a loser, like I'd lost control of my life," she remembered. "I was the fattest woman in the room."

Emmy gold: Oprah poses for the cameras after winning the Emmy for Outstanding Talk Show Host in 1992.

For Oprah, overeating was caused by uncomfortable feelings. These feelings included nervousness, sadness, and fear. After the Emmy Awards, Oprah went to a spa in Telluride, Colorado, to lose weight. There she met personal trainer Bob Greene. Oprah liked Greene right away. He was warm and friendly. And he didn't have a TV, so he didn't know much about her. Oprah asked Greene to develop a fitness program for her.

Oprah lost more than ten pounds at the spa, thanks to eating a low-fat diet and following Greene's exercise program. She felt better than she had in years. Oprah talked Bob Greene into moving to Chicago to be her personal trainer. His job would be to help her get in shape. Greene took the job.

Greene made sure that Oprah began her fitness program slowly. At first, she walked each day. She worked her way up to jogging three

Working out: Oprah and her trainer, Bob Greene, are ready for a workout.

miles a day, then eight miles a day. She worked out six days a week. When she went on vacation, Greene went with her. He was as dedicated to Oprah's fitness as she was. A few months later, Oprah completed a thirteen-mile race in San Diego, California.

The main goal of her new fitness program was good health, not just losing weight. She also got support from her personal chef, Rosie Daley. Daley kept Oprah on a diet of delicious, low-fat food. By 1993 Oprah had lost almost ninety pounds.

Meanwhile, Oprah continued to have great success with her show. Every television season, it was the number-one-rated talk show.

Millions of people around the United States watched it. Millions more tuned in worldwide.

On February 10, 1993, Oprah interviewed the singer Michael Jackson. Jackson is famous for disliking to be personally interviewed. About 62 million people—a bit more than the entire population of France—tuned in to this one show.

Healthy helper: Rosie Daley *(above)* helped Oprah eat better by carefully planning and preparing meals that tasted good and were nutritious.

Helping Others

In 1994 Oprah and Daley published *In the Kitchen with Rosie*. It was a cookbook of low-fat recipes by Daley. The day after Oprah talked about the book on her show, it sold at a record-breaking rate. It remained a best-seller for almost a year.

Oprah found joy in helping others to achieve success. In 1993 Deepak Chopra, a doctor from India, appeared on Oprah's show. Soon after, Chopra's book *Ageless Body, Timeless Mind* shot to the top of the best-seller lists.

One of Oprah's nicknames is Deepak Oprah. This is a word play on Deepak Chopra, whom she admires.

In 1994 Oprah found a different way to help people. She hosted an event to raise money for people in need. Her event was an auction of fancy clothing and shoes she had worn. It was held at Chicago's Hyatt Regency Hotel. One woman who went to the auction was a poor, single mother. She could only afford a five-dollar pair of shoes that were size ten. She wouldn't be able to wear the shoes, since her feet were size seven. But she wanted the shoes anyway. Later, the woman met Oprah after attending one of her shows. She told Oprah, "Sometimes I go in the closet when I'm feeling down and I stand in your shoes." "That story makes me want to weep," said Oprah. "It makes me think I must be doing something right."

The ratings for *The Oprah Winfrey Show* continued to be high. Still, Oprah looked for ways to make her show even better. She was tired of doing shows about damaged families, fighting relatives, and messed-up lives.

Ready to race: As part of her ongoing effort to lead an active life, Oprah trained to run in a marathon. Stedman was there to see her off.

"I was in the middle of a show with some [racist

people such as] white supremacists, skinheads, Ku Klux Klan members," Oprah remembered, "and I just had a flash, I thought, 'This is doing nobody any good—nobody.' I had [told myself], 'Oh, people need to know that these kinds of people are out here.' I won't do it anymore."

Oprah preferred to uplift and inspire viewers. In May 1995, she launched a six-week series on her show called "Get Movin' with Oprah." With the series, she hoped to help viewers get into fitness and exercise.

December 12, 1996

Has Oprah saved books?

From the Pages of USA TODAY

Once upon a time, books were hand sold, as they say in publishing. A bookstore owner would recommend a novel to a customer whose interest may have already been tickled by good reviews or praise from a friend.

TV personality Oprah Winfrey, however, moves books not copy by copy but rather truckload by truckload. Launched Sept. 17, Winfrey's on-air book club has emerged as an unprecedented force in thrusting serious fiction to the very top of the best-seller charts. Moreover, her club seems to slake a thirst for community in our isolated culture.

"I've never seen anything like this," comments Andrew Graves, co-owner of The Happy Bookseller, in Columbia, S.C. "As soon as Oprah Winfrey mentions a book on her show (as part of her book club), it becomes an instant best seller." He notes that the book club brings to the store new customers who are primarily women. Nothing else—no book review or media appearance—has equaled Winfrey's ability to popularize reading.

Oprah's Book Club

She also wanted to share her love of books with her viewers. "What a difference it makes in your world to go into some other life. It's what I love most. I'm reading always to leave myself . . . behind," said Oprah. "That's what reading is. You get to leave."

In 1996 Oprah started a reading group, Oprah's Book Club. On her show, she assigned a book for viewers to read. A month later, book club members would tune in for a talk with the author of the book.

"It's made books hip, and how could that be a bad thing?" asks Jacquelyn Mitchard, the author of *The Deep End of the Ocean*, Winfrey's first selection. Mitchard's first novel, about a 3-year-old abducted from a hotel lobby, did well before the show in terms of reviews and sales. But Winfrey's admiration made it a household name to her audience, estimated to be 15 million viewers daily.

With the book club, "she's really talked about books she herself has read and loved," says Viking director of publicity Patti Kelly, who handled *The Deep End of the Ocean* publicity campaign. Moreover, book clubs offer a sense of community in our isolated society, particularly to viewers of daytime TV who may lack the community of a workplace. "She's asking her audience to be part of something that means a great deal to her," Kelly says.

"Not only is she getting people to buy books," comments literary agent Aaron Priest, a 37-year veteran of publishing, "but she's getting people to buy books who usually don't buy books. . . . She's not preaching to the converted."

Once in the habit of book buying, a new customer may eventually branch out beyond Winfrey-recommended titles and Winfrey-created best sellers. This ability to tap into a virgin customer base sends publishers and booksellers into a froth because 1996 book sales have been sluggish. Indeed, the No. 1 question asked by publishers is: How do we get our book selected for Oprah's book club?

Well, they can forget "sending me boxes of books I don't want," Winfrey says. She chooses only books that "I have been emotionally moved by, books that I have loved." She reiterates that she wants to keep the book club "as pure as possible."

—Deirdre Donahue, December 12, 1996

In the club: Jacquelyn Mitchard *(above)* is the author of Oprah's first book club selection.

Oprah's first book club selection was *The Deep End of the Ocean.* The novel is about a family learning to live with the disappearance of a child. The book's author was Jacquelyn Mitchard. Mitchard saw that many of the books—and authors—later chosen for the book club had things in common. "All of the authors that she has picked for the book club were lonely children whose refuge was in books," Mitchard remarked. "Oprah is clearly in that club."

Oprah's Book Club was a hit right from the start. It helped boost the show's audience to nearly twenty million viewers. And the viewers bought the books that Oprah recommended. Book sales soared. The popularity of book clubs increased too. People across the country formed their own book clubs.

Book publishers were not prepared at first for the huge demand created by Oprah's show and book club. Her impact on book sales was called the Oprah phenomenon. It was the biggest change to hit the publishing industry in fifteen years, according to Philip Pfeffer, chief executive officer of the Borders bookstore chain. "Oprah Winfrey has been able to generate interest in reading through her book club," Pfeffer said. "The thing that's amazing to me is Oprah Winfrey airs at 4 P.M. The show is not watched by what we consider our [regular customers]. But Oprah's viewers go out and buy the books featured on the show."

Great writer: Toni Morrison *(above)* is one of Oprah's favorite writers. Oprah invited her to be part of her book club from the beginning.

Oprah also asked well-known writers to be part of the book club. These writers included Toni Morrison, the author of award-winning books such as *Song of Solomon* and *Beloved*. Oprah called Morrison "the greatest living American writer, male or female, white or black."

In 1996 Oprah talked about a book on her show that she herself had a part in creating. The book was *Make the Connection: Ten Steps to a Better Body—and a Better Life*. In it, Oprah discusses her struggles with weight loss. She and her personal trainer Bob Greene, describe a day-by-day fitness plan, using a positive, self-loving approach.

"I love this book because for so many years I struggled and wanted to be Diana Ross," Oprah said. "Then I realized no matter what I did I was not gonna have Diana's thighs! I realized that I just have to settle into what is the best body for me."

Oprah was learning to love herself more—and feel joy in her life. "I used to say I didn't have time to experience joy. I had too much to do," she said. "But I started to be aware of the life I'm living. . . . Now when we're running, I smell the jasmine; I notice when there's a pack of butterflies."

www.usatoday.com

USA TODAY

CHAPTER EIGHT

Presidential attention: Oprah greets President Bill Clinton after the president's Call to Action meeting in Philadelphia in 1997. Former presidents Gerald Ford *(left)* and George H. W. Bush *(seated, third from right)*, as well as former First Lady Nancy Reagan *(seated at right)* also attended the affair.

A Woman with Wings

In 1997 Oprah started Oprah's Angel Network. The goal of this charity was simply to make the world a better place to live. It would give college scholarships to fifty young people a year, chosen by the Boys and Girls Clubs of America. Each young person receives a twenty-five thousand dollar college scholarship.

Oprah also asked viewers to create their own "mini-miracle." They could do this by donating their spare change to the "world's largest piggy bank." With the money, Oprah planned to build more than two hundred "Oprah Houses" for Habitat for Humanity. Habitat for Humanity is a group that helps poor families build good houses. The houses are priced low enough that the families can own them.

By the summer of 2000, Oprah's Angel Network had collected more than $35 million.

Oprah's efforts continued in 1997. Harpo began production on a series of high-quality made-for-television movies titled Oprah Winfrey Presents. Harpo Productions broadcast the TV films over the next three years. The first of these movies—*Before Women Had Wings*, about a poor, abused girl named Bird Johnson—aired in November 1997. The film is based on the novel by Connie May Fowler and starred Oprah and Ellen Barkin. In February 1998, *The Wedding* aired. Another film in the series was *Tuesdays with Morrie*, the true story of a man's weekly visits with his dying former teacher.

Costars: Oprah hugs *Before Women Had Wings* costar Tina Majorino, who played Bird Johnson.

Also in 1997, Oprah released a videotape version of the book *Making the Connection* called *Oprah: Make the Connection*. She said the video was "about how to take control of your life. I am now about trying to convince people to stop wasting time. I know it's hard because it's much easier to want to believe there's some kind of magic fix coming along."

Oprah was always looking for ways to make her talk show more lively and interesting. In mid-1997, she made an announcement to her TV audience. She said that she would be taping an upcoming Oprah's Book Club show at the home of poet and novelist Maya Angelou.

IN FOCUS

Oprah's Favorites

Oprah has been a thirsty reader her entire life. She has long been drawn to female characters who get through hard times. Some of her favorite authors include:

Maya Angelou (born 1928), the author of *I Know Why the Caged Bird Sings*. This first part of Angelou's autobiography traces her life in the 1930s and 1940s. Although Angelou begins as an insecure girl, she experiences many trials that make her into a self-assured young woman.

Toni Morrison (born 1931), the author of *Beloved*. This dark and powerful novel addresses the long-term effects of slavery on a woman named Sethe. Oprah played Sethe in the 1998 movie version.

Alice Walker (born 1944), the author of *The Color Purple*. This novel describes the pain suffered by Celie, the main character, and her transformation. Another character, Sofia, doesn't back down from racism and abuse. Oprah played Sofia in the movie version.

Margaret Walker (1915–1998), the author of *Jubilee*. This story about a slave named Vyry before, during, and after the Civil War shares the details of black life in the South. Despite much suffering, Vyry survives and forgives those who have hurt her.

Angelou had recently released a new nonfiction book, *The Heart of a Woman*. Oprah has called her "the woman who has had, undoubtedly, the greatest influence on my life."

Influential: Maya Angelou's poetry and prose have been very influential in Oprah's life. Oprah chose one of Maya's books for her book club in 1997.

Oprah had forgotten to get Maya's permission to hold the book club party. When Oprah made the announcement, Maya was watching the show at home. She started laughing. She shouted at the television, "But you haven't spoken to me!"

Oprah won her over. In June 1997, Maya threw an on-the-air book club pajama party at her home in Winston-Salem, North Carolina. Maya, Oprah, and four other women, all wearing comfy pajamas, discussed *The Heart of a Woman*. Afterward, Maya served a big, home-cooked meal.

Trouble in Texas

Oprah worked hard to make her show full of useful information. After a while, that got her in trouble. She ran an episode of *The Oprah Winfrey Show* that was called "Dangerous Food." On the show, Oprah's guests talked about the risks of mad cow disease. This rare disease affects the brain. It was said to come from eating beef. At the time, there had not been a case of it in the United States.

At one point in the show, a vegetarian activist talked about the dangers of the disease. Oprah blurted out, "It has just stopped me cold from eating another burger."

Oprah's comment made some people very angry, especially a group of Texas cattle ranchers. They filed a lawsuit against Oprah. They claimed that her words had harmed their image. They said her statement had cost the cattle industry millions of dollars.

In January 1998, Oprah traveled to Amarillo, Texas, for the trial. She brought her staff from Harpo Productions with her. Oprah appeared in court every day for the trial, and then taped her talk show after leaving the courthouse.

Oprah remained calm throughout the trial. After six weeks, the Texas jury found that Oprah was not responsible for damage to the beef industry. All charges against her were dropped.

Amarillo, Texas: Oprah celebrates after winning the lawsuit brought against her by cattle ranchers.

"Free speech not only lives, it rocks!" Oprah happily announced to her many fans at the end of the trial. "I will continue to use my voice," she said. "I believed from the beginning that this was an attempt to muzzle that voice. And I come from a people who have struggled and died in order to have a voice in this country, and I refuse to be muzzled."

USA TODAY Snapshots®

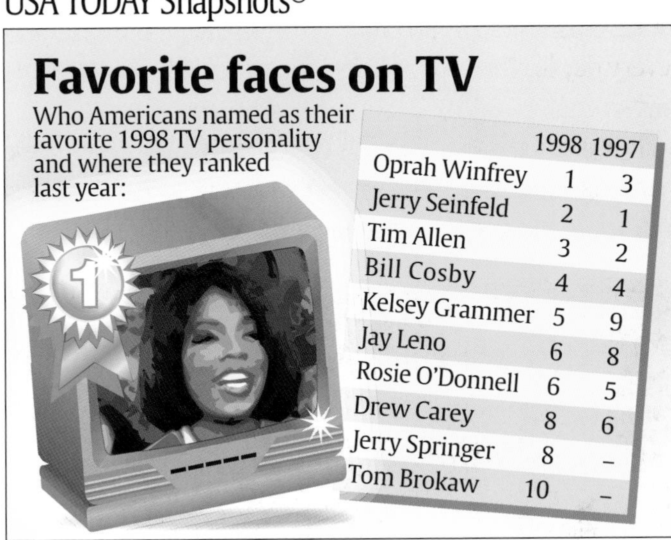

Favorite faces on TV

Who Americans named as their favorite 1998 TV personality and where they ranked last year:

	1998	1997
Oprah Winfrey	1	3
Jerry Seinfeld	2	1
Tim Allen	3	2
Bill Cosby	4	4
Kelsey Grammer	5	9
Jay Leno	6	8
Rosie O'Donnell	6	5
Drew Carey	8	6
Jerry Springer	8	–
Tom Brokaw	10	–

Source: Harris Poll

By Anne R. Carey and Gary Visgaitis, USA TODAY, 1998

Beloved

Oprah has always felt a strong sense of pride in her African American heritage. In 1997 she started a new project that meant a lot to her. She would star in the movie version of *Beloved*, a novel by Toni Morrison.

The film was directed by Jonathan Demme. Oprah played Sethe, an escaped slave living on a farm in Ohio in 1873. Sethe is haunted by her memories of being a slave on the Sweet Home plantation. She is also haunted by the ghost of her baby daughter, Beloved. Sethe is reunited with another ex-slave from Sweet Home, Paul D, played by Danny Glover.

Oprah knew that making the film wasn't going to be easy. But she didn't know just how hard it would be to play the role of Sethe. She struggled to understand the feelings that come from slavery.

"I thought I knew it," she said. But she didn't understand the feelings as well as she thought she did. "During the process of doing *Beloved*, for the first time, I went to the knowing place," she said.

Beloved: This still shows Danny Glover and Oprah while filming *Beloved*, which was produced by Oprah's production company.

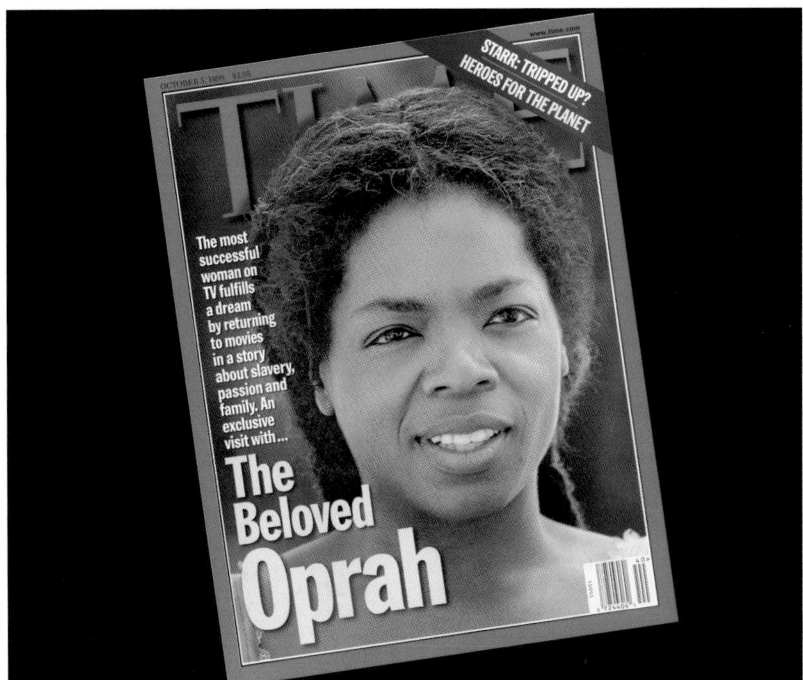

Cover girl: Oprah appeared on the October 5, 1998, issue of *Time* magazine in connection with *Beloved.*

Oprah wanted to prepare for her film role and get a closer sense of what it was like to be a slave. She was dumped at a spot in the Maryland woods. The spot used to be part of the Underground Railroad, a route that runaway slaves had traveled to escape slavery. White men acting the part of slave trackers called her names. Oprah felt strong and unafraid at first. But then she broke down.

"I became hysterical," Oprah said. "It was raw, raw, raw pain," Oprah went on. "I went to the darkest place, and I saw the light. And I thought, 'So this is where I come from.'"

The experience of making *Beloved* stayed with Oprah long after filming was over. "The first time I saw [the film], I thought they were going to have to carry me out," she said. "Every single image caused such intense, deeply felt emotions."

Beloved was released in movie theaters in October 1998. While the film received good reviews, it did not sell many tickets. Oprah was disappointed that so few people went to the movie. But she had grown as a person by making the movie. She had also formed a solid bond with the book's author, Toni Morrison. Oprah invited her friend to her farm in Indiana.

October 16, 1998

Will fans boost their 'Beloved' Winfrey's film?

From the Pages of USA TODAY

When the movie *Beloved* opens today, Oprah Winfrey may find out just how powerful she is. The adaptation of Toni Morrison's Pulitzer Prize-winning novel, which Winfrey produced and stars in, has gained critical acclaim and Oscar buzz.

But even the talk show queen whose book club creates best sellers could have trouble enticing the masses to buy tickets to a long, emotionally taxing film. (The $53 million *Beloved* runs nearly three hours and graphically examines the trauma of slavery.)

"It is a difficult sell," says Paul Dergarabedian of box-office tracking firm Exhibitor Relations. "How are you going to get audiences into theaters when you say flat out, 'This is a parable about slavery?'"

Disney hopes the answer is simple: Oprah. She's the centerpiece of the studio's $30 million marketing campaign.

"Oprah has the capability to take material such as literature or art and bring it to an everyday audience," says Disney spokeswoman Terry Curtin. "Her audience

Morrison was impressed by Oprah's book-filled home. "Except for other writers', I have very seldom seen a home with so many books—all kinds of books, handled and read books," said Morrison.

Besides reading, Oprah enjoyed spending time with friends and with Stedman. "I decided that I wanted to have more fun in my life, and I've been having a ball," she said in 1998.

really listens to what she recommends. She is in a unique position, more than anybody in Hollywood, to get people interested."

"She is the linchpin to the marketing of the film," says David Davis, entertainment analyst for the investment banking firm of Houlihan Lokey Howard & Zukin. "She has such a loyal following that her fans are actually the type that puts money on the table."

Things look pretty good for *Beloved*, at least for its first weekend. "People from (Winfrey's) television audience will go. There is no question about that," he says. "But the question is: What will they tell their friends the next day?"

—Josh Chetwynd,
October 16, 1998

Premiere: Toni Morrison *(left)* and Oprah attend the premiere of *Beloved* in October 1998.

www.usatoday.com

USA TODAY

CHAPTER NINE

Expanding an empire: In 2000 Oprah celebrated the launch of *O: The Oprah Magazine*.

The Sky Is the Limit

Oprah and *The Oprah Winfrey Show* had been winning Daytime Emmy Awards almost every year. In 1998 Oprah received a Daytime Emmy Award for lifetime achievement. She decided that she would take her name off the Daytime Emmy Award list forever. She figured that there wasn't much left after winning a lifetime award.

In the fall of 1998, Oprah began a new season of her show. She called the new season Change Your Life TV. One guest was John Gray, author of the best-selling self-help book *Men Are from Mars, Women Are from Venus*. Gray stresses that men and women handle emotions differently. On the show, he encouraged couples to work out their problems in helpful, useful, creative ways. Oprah also added a new part to the show called "Remembering Your Spirit." In it, she showed how viewers could take time for themselves. She talked about how people could take care of their spiritual lives.

Millions of viewers, mostly women, tune in to *The Oprah Winfrey Show* each week. It remains the highest-rated talk show in history. About twenty-five thousand letters and e-mails arrive at Harpo Productions each week. *The Oprah Winfrey Show* is seen in dozens of countries, including South Africa, China, Japan, and Israel. Oprah is the wealthiest female entertainer in the world.

USA TODAY Snapshots®

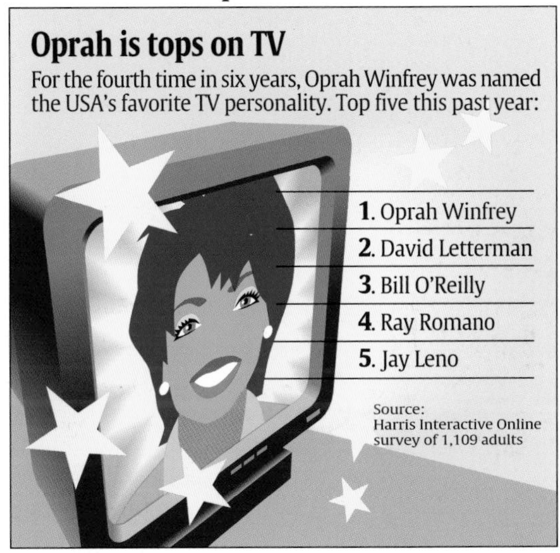

By Joseph Popiolkowski and Sam Ward, USA TODAY, 2004

Media Superwoman

Newsweek calls Oprah Winfrey "one of the most powerful brand names in the entertainment industry"—meaning that anything with the name "Oprah" on it is bound to be a success.

In May 2000, she teamed up with Hearst Magazines to start yet another new project—her own magazine. *O: The Oprah Magazine* features upbeat self-improvement articles and inspirational stories. The first issue of *O* came out in mid-2000. It sold 1.1 million copies.

January 18, 2001

O sister, where art thou?

From the Pages of USA TODAY

Oh! Or better yet, wow!

That's what the magazine industry is saying about *O*, Oprah Winfrey's start-up magazine, which in just eight issues has far surpassed the wildest dreams of all involved.

Some facts and figures: Advertisers are guaranteed a circulation of 1.3 million, a figure that will go up to 1.6 million this spring. Subscriptions alone stand at 1.6 million. Newsstand sales are 1.2 million.

"So you've already got over 2.5 million people buying this magazine every month," says Debra Shriver, an executive at Hearst, the media giant that publishes the talk-show host's magazine. Some 300,000 subscriptions were given as holiday gifts alone. By comparison, *Martha Stewart Living*, after almost 10 years, has 1.9 million subscribers.

The magazine, an inspirational self-help publication for women to help them lead their best lives, went monthly after only two issues, and the first issues were reprinted because they sold out almost immediately. One in three of those who did pick up the inaugural issue decided to become subscribers. Magazine industry watchers say a 33% return is unheard of.

But the proof is always in the advertising. When *Living* launched in 1991, it had 226 ad pages in the first six issues, with revenues of $4.6 million. *O* had, in its first six issues, 905 ad pages, with revenues of $50.9 million. A well-established monthly magazine hopes to get 1,000 ad pages a year.

It's no secret that Oprah is a phenomenon. "Everything she touches turns to gold," says Melissa Pordy of Zenith Media, an ad buying service in New York. With Oprah right on the cover, "the reader knows the journalism they're going to encounter inside."

—Craig Wilson, January 18, 2001

Oprah demands perfection from the *O* staff. "Look," she told the staff. "I know that to you guys the Oprah name is a brand. But for me, it's my life . . . and the way I behave and everything I stand for."

Each month, Oprah writes a column for the magazine. In the first issue, she wrote about her mission for the magazine. "How far can you grow?" she wrote. "What will it take for you to fulfill your potential? My hope is that this magazine will help you lead a more productive life."

Some critics say that Oprah acts too much like a preacher or a psychologist on her show and in the magazine. But millions of people continue to seek inspiration from Oprah. In June 2000, Oprah held her Personal Growth Summit. She brought the self-help seminar to four cities. "I'm not here to preach to anyone about how to run your life," she told one crowd. "I just know what worked for me and I'm here to share it." She followed it up with sold-out "Live Your Best Life" workshops in 2001.

Time with Oprah: A South African woman reads an issue of *O* while getting her hair done. The magazine appeals to women and men around the world.

July 2, 2001

Live your best life, with Oprah

From the Pages of USA TODAY

Celebrity worship ranks as one of the media's more toxic waste products. For Oprah Winfrey, I'm making an exception. After attending her all-day "Live Your Best Life" workshop Saturday in Baltimore, I was impressed not so much by Winfrey but by the effect she had on some of the 1,600 attendees.

"I feel so pumped up and ready to conquer the world," said Ann Adams, 38. "Oprah has the ability to really connect with women: rich, poor, white, black. . . . She is able to get people over the bridge and past their obstacles."

"I'm charged," said Jackie Maynard, 47. "She's it. I love her."

Winfrey has already changed Maynard's life. For the past four years, Maynard has been mentoring a little girl once a week because Winfrey stresses the importance of serving others.

First with her syndicated talk show, then her year-and-a-half-old magazine, *O*, and now with these workshops, Winfrey wants to infuse middle America's soul with a non-sectarian spirituality. She urges her fans to meditate, focus on their dreams, write in journals and breathe deeply. Most of all she wants us to listen to that inner voice that has since time began directed human beings away from life's distracting chatter and toward a sense of the divine, the good and the true.

Although some might consider the [workshops] a New Age babblefest promoting unattainable dreams and self-absorption, Winfrey is not lacking for followers. The $185 tickets to the Baltimore event sold out in 47 minutes. Sponsored by *O*, which has a circulation of 2.5 million, three earlier "Live Your Best Life" events in Raleigh-Durham, Minneapolis and San Francisco in June also sold out immediately.

—Deirdre Donahue, July 2, 2001

"Oprah is a good mentor for us black women," said Janet Graham, a woman who had gone to a seminar. She was a thirty-six-year-old counselor for abused women and children. "She's been through a lot and nothing's been handed to her. . . . It's inspiring. How big do you dream, especially if you've never seen anyone who looks like you reach that high? Because of her, other women reach higher."

Oprah continues to give not only her time to people but her money as well. In July 2000, she wrote a check for $10 million to A Better Chance. The organization places gifted minority students in top schools across the country. In 2002 she gave fifty thousand Christmas gifts to kids in South Africa, a country recovering from years of harsh government. She later started working on building schools there.

Oprah still struggles with very human issues, even though her career has been a huge success. One issue is her weight. "I eat when I'm happy, I eat when I'm sad, I eat when I'm depressed," Oprah says. "I eat when I can't decide am I happy, depressed or sad. I say, 'Let me have some potato chips and decide.'"

Honors: In 2002 Oprah was awarded the Bob Hope Humanitarian Award for her social and cultural impact through the medium of television.

Oprah's money doesn't protect her from problems. "I am so rich I cannot believe it," Oprah said at a Personal Growth Summit meeting. But, she added, "Every issue y'all have had, I've had it too."

Forbes, a financial magazine, listed Oprah Winfrey as the first African American woman to become a billionaire.

Keeping Things Fresh

Oprah's energy seemed to run low in 2002. In March of that year, she said she would stop doing her show after the 2005–2006 season. The next month, she stopped doing her book club.

However, in May 2003, she seemed to get her groove back. She signed a contract to continue doing *The Oprah Winfrey Show* through the 2007–2008 season. In June 2003, she started the book club again.

Family: Oprah attends a film opening in Nashville with Stedman, her father *(center)*, and his second wife *(left)* in 2003.

June 19, 2003

'East of Eden' heralds Oprah's return

From the Pages of USA TODAY

Sitting under the oaks at her home last summer in Santa Barbara, Calif., Oprah Winfrey read John Steinbeck's retelling of the Cain and Abel tragedy, *East of Eden*.

She wished she hadn't ended the enormously successful book club she had started in 1996 and stopped in April 2002 after selecting 48 books. She called her friends to rave about the novel but found it was "not as much fun as telling a million people."

On Wednesday, she relaunched Oprah's Book Club. The new club will be more interactive. Readers can register at oprah.com and receive a weekly e-mail from Winfrey at no charge. There also will be online discussions and audio segments of Winfrey reading favorite passages. Living and dead writers will be considered as well as foreign authors.

For the new printing of *East of Eden*, the book is wrapped in a band that says: "The Book That Brought Oprah's Book Club Back." Winfrey says she is happy that the $16 Penguin paperback is less expensive than a hardcover. The 600,000 copies shipped to bookstores were kept in sealed cartons until Wednesday.

–Deirdre Donahue, June 19, 2003

And she added *Oprah after the Show*, an informal time for the audience and the guests to talk—but still in front of the cameras. Her Live Your Best Life speaking tour evolved in 2003 into an interactive multimedia workshop where visitors could experience Oprah's personal style as well as tackle life-changing questions. Based on the success of *O*, Oprah launched *O at Home* in 2004, a newsstand-only magazine that comes out four times a year. It focuses on ways readers can shape and design their homes to reflect their passions and personalities. Supporting these many ventures is her elaborate website, oprah.com, which millions of people visit per month.

Through her TV show and website, she started Oprah's Child Predator Watch List in 2005. It shows escaped convicted child predators and offers a reward for help in capturing them. (Seven fugitives had been captured as of late 2007.) Oprah next brought *The Color Purple* to a whole new audience by producing the story as a Broadway musical. The show received mixed reviews but got a lot of support from Oprah through her TV show. After closing in New York, the musical began a nationwide tour. She also aided the victims of Hurricane Katrina by spearheading efforts to help the survivors rebuild their lives.

Never to stay still for long, Oprah then launched *Oprah & Friends*, a radio show featuring personalities from her show and magazine,

Broadway: Oprah stands onstage with author Alice Walker *(left)*, producer Scott Sanders *(second from left)*, and actress LaChanze *(right)* following the curtain call of the opening night of *The Color Purple* on Broadway in New York.

such as Gayle King, Bob Greene, and Marianne Williamson. Debuting in September 2006, the show has regular segments on current events, health, self-improvement, books, and home style. One part of the show gives listeners a chance to talk directly with Oprah.

Oprah described January 2, 2007, as the "proudest, greatest day of my life." She was opening the Oprah Winfrey Leadership Academy for Girls in Henley-on-Klip, South Africa. On hand for the ceremony were former South African president Nelson Mandela, as well as celebrities Mary J. Blige, Tina Turner, Spike Lee, and Sidney Poitier. Oprah has plans for building additional schools in other parts of Africa.

Helping out: Oprah comforts a woman who was separated from her relatives during Hurricane Katrina in 2005.

USA TODAY Snapshots®

By Darryl Haralson and Joni Alexander, USA TODAY, 2005

IN FOCUS

A School in Johannesburg

In 2002 Oprah Winfrey had the chance to meet Nelson Mandela, the former president of South Africa who had led his country through its first years as a multiracial democracy. She asked him what gift she could give to South Africa. Mandela told her to build a school.

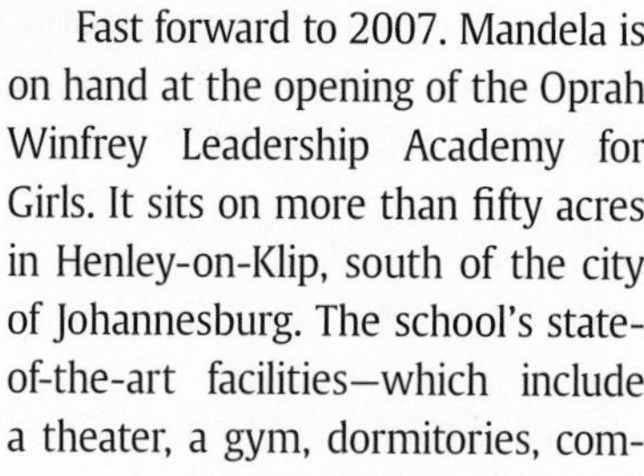

Fast forward to 2007. Mandela is on hand at the opening of the Oprah Winfrey Leadership Academy for Girls. It sits on more than fifty acres in Henley-on-Klip, south of the city of Johannesburg. The school's state-of-the-art facilities—which include a theater, a gym, dormitories, computer and science labs, and a library—cost Oprah more than $40 million to build.

Girls chosen to live at the boarding school had to show academic excellence as well as leadership skills. Their families had to be from a low-income bracket, making less than $800 per month. The first group of girls numbered more than 150, but eventually the school will accommodate 450 students in grades seven through twelve.

South Africa: Oprah and Nelson Mandela *(left)* break ground at the Oprah Winfrey Leadership Academy for Girls in South Africa.

Fans of Oprah praised her for her big gift and her ongoing interest in education. Detractors worried that the girls, who come from all over South Africa, will forget their roots in their communities. Late in 2007, allegations of child abuse surfaced at the school. The charges resulted in several staff being fired. Oprah was undaunted, however. She flew to the school and apologized to the parents and students. She provided counselors to the children and vowed to learn the lesson that "you have to be far more careful in choosing people to stand in the gap for you."

With her girls: Oprah meets with a prospective student *(top)*. Oprah selected each of the 150 girls in the first class of the leadership academy. *Bottom:* Oprah celebrates the opening of her school with its new students in 2007.

Moving in another direction, Oprah decided to lend her name, voice, and celebrity status to the presidential campaign of Illinois senator Barack Obama. It was her first endorsement of a political figure. In an interview on CNN with Larry King, she said, "I didn't know anybody well enough to be able to say, I believe in this person." But Obama and Oprah both live in Chicago, and she has known the senator and his wife for several years.

First, she helped Obama by hosting a fund-raising event at her

December 10, 2007

Huge crowds line up for Obama, Winfrey

From the Pages of USA TODAY

Linda Brown is still making up her mind about voting for Democratic presidential hopeful Barack Obama, but she's not undecided about his most famous backer: Oprah Winfrey.

"I watch her every day," said Brown, who was one of the first in line to see Winfrey and Obama at a rally here Sunday. How much weight does Winfrey's seal of approval carry? "Quite a bit," Brown said. "She would not endorse anyone who did not share her values."

At rallies in Iowa, South Carolina and New Hampshire, Winfrey and Obama drew huge crowds who lined up hours in advance and chanted the campaign's slogan, "Fired up, ready to go!" while they waited.

So great is Winfrey's appeal that the rally in South Carolina had to be moved from an 18,000-seat arena to a football stadium to accommodate the nearly 30,000 people who turned out Sunday.

home in California. She followed it up with a three-state visit in late 2007. Tickets to her appearances were in high demand, and tens of thousands filled the stadiums in Iowa, South Carolina, and New Hampshire to hear Oprah say she felt "compelled to . . . speak out for the man who I believe has a new vision for America." Not all her fans were in favor of her getting involved in politics, and some even said they'd stop watching her show. But Oprah said she was willing to risk their displeasure.

"I've never seen anything like it," said Dick Harpootlian, former South Carolina Democratic Party chairman. "People will go back to their communities to talk about what they saw here today. . . . I don't know we'll see anything like it again. It was amazing."

In Manchester, despite freezing temperatures and a forecast of snow and rain, the crowd—predominantly women—began lining up more than four hours before the evening rally. Some had taken the day off work to be there.

"I really respect her opinion," said Paulette Talkington, 54, from Franklin, N.H. She said she was so excited to see Winfrey she hadn't been able to sleep the night before. The fact that Winfrey is making her first political endorsement "speaks volumes to me."

Winfrey's popularity is such that she drew people to see Obama who otherwise might not have turned out. One of those reluctant voters, by her own admission, is Linda Clevesy, 47, of Barnstead. She came to the rally with her daughter Deanna, 17. "I'm . . . a little passive about these things," she said. For her, the draw was "Oprah. I can't lie. The celebrity . . . is very intriguing."

"When I heard she was coming I couldn't believe it," said Rita Montpelier, who took the day off from her job at a General Electric plant in Hooksett to come to the rally. "This is my first campaign speech I've ever listened to" in person, she said.

—Martha T. Moore, December 10, 2007

Campaigning: Oprah joined presidential candidate Barack Obama for a campaign stop in Des Moines, Iowa, in 2007.

Oprah got back to her TV roots in 2008 with the premiere of *Oprah's Big Give*, a reality show in which the contestants, called Big Givers, are given money and the names of people—all strangers with financial challenges—whom they are to help in a meaningful way. Judges determine which Givers have most creatively put their money and time to work and have made a difference in the life of a complete stranger. Each week someone is eliminated from the competition. The winning Giver gets $1 million from Oprah.

Taking her celebrity one step farther, Oprah signed with Discovery Communications to create her own network—the Oprah Winfrey Network, or OWN—in 2009. Harpo will develop programming for OWN that mirrors the types of subjects that Oprah talks about on her show. Her contract with King World to produce her show goes through 2011. She said it's possible new shows or reruns of her show could move to OWN.

January 16, 2008

Oprah gets her own cable network, launching in '09

From the Pages of USA TODAY

Oprah Winfrey is getting her own cable channel, called OWN: The Oprah Winfrey Network.

A deal announced Tuesday with Discovery Communications will create a 50-50 cable and Web venture. In the cashless transaction, Discovery will contribute its Discovery Health Channel, to be converted to OWN in late 2009 and simulcast in HD. Winfrey's company, Harpo, will kick in her website, Oprah.com.

Her goal is a network "that will inspire and entertain people around issues of money, weight, health, relationships, spirit, helping people to raise their children and give back, teaching people to be all that they can be in the world," said Winfrey, whose empire includes her TV show, Harpo Films and Oprah's Books.

Winfrey said that until her contract with CBS-owned King World Productions expires in 2011, she can't put her syndicated TV show or reruns on OWN. But she added, "Eventually that will happen, we hope."

—David Lieberman, January 16, 2008

Oprah does not get too proud. She doesn't see herself as a leader or a preacher or a teacher anymore. At heart, she doesn't think she's different from anyone else. "I'm just a voice trying to help people rediscover their best selves," she says. "All of us have that within us. [It's like] The Wizard of Oz, when Glinda, the Good Witch, tells Dorothy, 'You've always had it, my dear.' You've always had the power. Everyone has the power inside."

TIMELINE

1954 Oprah Winfrey is born on January 29 in Kosciusko, Mississippi. Her parents, Vernita Lee and Vernon Winfrey, are not married.

1958 Vernita leaves for Milwaukee, Wisconsin. Oprah remains with her grandmother, Hattie Mae Lee.

late 1950s Hattie Mae teaches Oprah to read. She recites Bible passages at Baptist church services.

1959 Oprah starts kindergarten but is quickly moved into first grade.

1960 Oprah joins her mother in Milwaukee. Oprah's half sister Patricia is born.

1962 Vernita sends Oprah to live with Vernon Winfrey in Nashville, Tennessee. She starts third grade at Wharton Elementary. Oprah's half brother Jeffrey is born.

1963 Oprah moves back to Milwaukee. She is raped by her cousin. Hattie Mae Lee dies in Mississippi.

mid-1960s Oprah is repeatedly sexually abused. She attends Lincoln Middle School in Milwaukee. A teacher named Gene Abrams helps Oprah transfer to Nicolet High School through the Upward Bound program.

1968 Oprah becomes pregnant. She exhibits wild behavior, and her mother sends her back to Nashville. Oprah gives birth prematurely. The baby dies. She starts tenth grade at East High School in Nashville.

1970 Oprah wins a speech contest sponsored by the Elks Club. The prize is a four-year college scholarship.

1971 Oprah wins the Miss Fire Prevention beauty contest, representing radio station WVOL. The station offers her part-time work as a news reader. She graduates from East High. She starts attending Tennessee State University.

1972 Oprah wins the Miss Black Tennessee beauty contest.

1973 WTVF-TV in Nashville hires Oprah to anchor its evening news show.

1976 Oprah accepts a job as news reporter for WJZ-TV in Baltimore, Maryland. While there, she meets Gayle King, another newscaster at the station.

1978 Oprah and Richard Sher cohost *People Are Talking*, a talk show on WJZ-TV.

1984 Oprah leaves WJZ-TV for WLS-TV in Chicago. She hosts *A.M. Chicago*.

1985 Because of Oprah's success, WLS-TV renames *A.M. Chicago The Oprah Winfrey Show*. Quincy Jones taps her to take the part of Sofia in the movie version of *The Color Purple*.

1986 Oprah is nominated for an Academy Award for her performance but doesn't win. She signs a deal with King World to broadcast *The Oprah Winfrey Show* nationwide. She starts her own production company, Harpo.

1987 Oprah wins her first Daytime Emmy Award for Outstanding Talk Show Host. She meets Stedman Graham.

1988 Harpo buys the rights to produce *The Oprah Winfrey Show*. Oprah goes on a strict diet and shows off her weight loss on her show.

1989 Oprah opens the Eccentric restaurant in Chicago. She buys a large farm in Rolling Prairie, Indiana. Her half brother dies of AIDS.

1991 Oprah speaks before the Senate Judiciary Committee about child abuse.

1992 Oprah wins her third Daytime Emmy for Outstanding Talk Show Host. Soon afterward, she goes to a spa where she meets Bob Greene. He becomes her personal trainer. Her personal chef, Rosie Daley, puts her on a low-fat diet.

1993 President Bill Clinton signs into law the National Child Protection Act, more popularly known as Oprah's Bill *(below)*. Through her efforts with Bob and Rosie, Oprah loses ninety pounds.

1994 Oprah and Rosie coauthor a cookbook called *In the Kitchen with Rosie*. It becomes a best-seller.

1996 Oprah starts Oprah's Book Club on her TV show. She and Bob Greene write *Make the Connection: Ten Steps to a Better Body—and a Better Life.*

1997 Oprah starts a charity called Oprah's Angel Network. It funds college scholarships, home building, and other activities for low-income people. Harpo produces made-for TV movies as part of Oprah Winfrey Presents. She starts filming the movie *Beloved.*

1998 After a show about mad cow disease, Oprah is accused of defaming the cattle industry by Texas cattlemen. Harpo is brought to trial in Amarillo, Texas, but all charges are dropped. *Beloved* is released to good reviews but low ticket sales.

2000 Oprah founds *O: The Oprah Magazine.*

2001 Oprah holds "Live Your Best Life" workshops around the country.

2003 Oprah signs up to keep doing her show through 2008. She adds *Oprah after the Show* to her TV lineup.

2004 Based on the popularity of *O*, Oprah launches *O at Home.*

2005 Oprah founds Oprah's Child Predator List on her website. She helps survivors of Hurricane Katrina.

2006 With Oprah's backing, *The Color Purple* becomes a Broadway musical. Oprah starts a radio show, *Oprah & Friends*, featuring people involved with her show.

2007 Oprah opens the Oprah Winfrey Leadership Academy for Girls in South Africa. Later, accusations of child abuse cause her to fire several staff. She supports Illinois senator Barack Obama's bid for the U.S. presidency.

2008 *Oprah's Big Give*, a reality show, premieres. She signs with Discovery Communications to create her own network—the Oprah Winfrey Network (OWN)—in 2009.

GLOSSARY

affirmative action: a U.S. government effort to improve the chances that a minority person or a woman can get a good job and a good education

Baptist: a member of a large Protestant Christian group that believes only mature church members can make the decision to be baptized (or to join the church)

Black Power: a point of view that formed in the 1960s to push for African Americans to create their own political, economic, and cultural systems

Boys and Girls Clubs of America: a not-for-profit youth group that tries to help kids from low-income backgrounds

cable television: a television service in which signals from television stations are sent into the homes of paying customers by way of a cable or wire

child predator: a person who is convicted of a criminal sexual offense against a victim who is aged thirteen or younger

civil rights movement: a group that joins together to push for freedom and equal treatment of all members of society under the law

cohost: to be in charge of a TV show, radio show, or other entertainment with another person

Elks Club: a U.S. charity that gives millions of dollars to study kid-related diseases and to send kids to college

Emmy Awards: a set of annual awards that honor the best performances, writing, and production on television

endorsement: a promotional statement or action by someone famous for someone or something. A famous person might endorse a product, a charity, or a person running for office.

Habitat for Humanity: a Christian, not-for-profit group that builds quality, low-cost housing in the United States and around the world for people of any—or no—religion

mad cow disease: a fatal brain illness in cattle that can be picked up by humans who eat beef containing the disease

media: newspapers, television, radio, and the Internet that are used to get information to a large number of people at once

national syndication: a means of selling TV programs directly to local stations throughout the United States

plantation: a large farm usually in a warm climate. In the 1700s and up to the mid-1800s, plantations in the southern United States typically used slave labor.

racial prejudice: an opinion formed unfairly about an ethnic group. Racial prejudice can lead to racial segregation, or the practice of keeping ethnic groups apart.

reality show: a television or radio show that deals with real people in real situations

Underground Railroad: a secret network of people, routes, and safe houses that helped escaped slaves find their way out of the South before the Civil War

U.S. Supreme Court: the highest court in the United States

Global attention: Oprah gets her picture taken with one of her many fans.

SOURCE NOTES

4 Oprah Winfrey, "Oprah Winfrey Interview: Entertainment Executive," *Academy of Achievement*, February 21, 1991, http://www.achievement.org/autodoc/page/win0int-1 (June 4, 2004).

7 Ron Stodghill, "Daring to Go There," *Time*, October 5, 1998, 80.

8 Winfrey, "Oprah Winfrey Interview: Entertainment Executive."

9 Ibid.

9 Marilyn Johnson, "Oprah Winfrey," *Life*, September 1997, 44.

9 Audreen Buffalo, *Meet Oprah Winfrey* (New York: Random House, 1993), 27–28.

10 Johnson, 44.

11 Jenny Allen, "Oprah Winfrey," *US Weekly*, June 12, 2000, 67.

13 Johnson, 44.

13 Winfrey, "Oprah Winfrey Interview: Entertainment Executive."

14 "That's the Wonderful Thing about Great Teachers: Every One Is an Inspiration to Somebody," *CTA Quest*, n.d., http://www.ctaquest.org/quest_quest/1_oprah/oprah.html (September 1, 2000).

14 "Oprah Winfrey: Entertainment Executive."

15 "Oprah Winfrey: Entertainment Executive."

18 John Culhane, "Oprah Winfrey: How Truth Changed Her Life," *Reader's Digest*, February 1989, 102.

19 William Ernest Henley, *Invictus*, available online at "Invictus," *Wikipedia*, April 11, 2008, http://en.wikipedia.org/wiki/Invictus (May 3, 2008).

20 Johnson, 44.

21 Winfrey, "Oprah Winfrey Interview: Entertainment Executive."

21 Norman King, *Everybody Loves Oprah* (New York: William Morrow and Co., 1987), 48.

22 Ibid., 49.

26 Culhane, 103.

27 Johnson, 44.

27 King, 62.

28 Winfrey, "Oprah Winfrey Interview: Entertainment Executive."

28–29 Ibid.

29 Ibid.

30 Ibid.

30 King, 63.
30 Winfrey, "Oprah Winfrey Interview: Entertainment Executive."
31 King, 75.
33 Audrey Edwards, "Oprah Winfrey, Stealing the Show," *Essence*, October 1986, 52.
35 King, 78
35 Ibid., 79.
36–37 Winfrey, "Oprah Winfrey Interview: Entertainment Executive."
39 Ibid.
39–40 Ibid.
40–41 Ibid.
42 Allen, 67.
42 Winfrey, "Oprah Winfrey Interview: Entertainment Executive."
43 A&E Television Networks, "Phil Donahue Biography," *Biography.com*, 2003, http://www.biography.com/search/article.do?id=9542194&page (May 3, 2008).
45 *Oprah Winfrey: Heart of the Matter*, VHS (ABC for A&E Networks, 1999).
45 Ibid.
46 Winfrey, "Oprah Winfrey Interview: Entertainment Executive."
48 Johnson, 44.
48 Winfrey, "Oprah Winfrey Interview: Entertainment Executive."
48 Johnson, 44.
49 David Ansen, "We Shall Overcome," *Newsweek*, December 30, 1985, 60.
50 Leslie Rubenstein, "Oprah! Thriving on Faith," *McCall's*, December 1987, 140.
51 *Good Housekeeping*, "Girlfriends Are Forever," May 2000, 110.
52 Winfrey, "Oprah Winfrey Interview: Entertainment Executive."
52 *Oprah Winfrey: Heart of the Matter.*
53 Ibid.
57 Laura B. Randolph, "Oprah Opens Up about Her Weight, Her Wedding and Why She Withheld the Book," *Ebony*, October 1993, 130.
59 Ibid.
60 Pearl Cleage, "Walking in the Light," *Essence*, June 1991, 48.
61 Winfrey, "Oprah Winfrey Interview: Entertainment Executive."

62–62 Ibid.

63 Winfrey, "Oprah Winfrey Interview: Entertainment Executive."

64 Joanna Powell, "I Was Trying to Fill Something Deeper," *Good Housekeeping*, October 1996, 80.

64 Ibid.

67 Lisa Russell and Cindy Dampier, "Oprah Winfrey," *People Weekly*, March 15, 1999, 143.

67–68 Winfrey, "Oprah Winfrey Interview: Entertainment Executive."

69 Johnson, 44.

70 Ibid.

70 Arthur Bridgeforth Jr., "Internet, Oprah, Enliven Sluggish Book Industry," *Crain's Detroit Business*, January 18, 1999, 27.

71 Johnson, 44.

71 Powell, 80.

71 Ibid.

74 *Jet*, "Oprah Winfrey Gives Her Weight Loss Tips in New Video, 'Oprah: Make the Connection,'" October 20, 1997, 23.

75 Johnson, 44.

75 Ibid.

76 Laurel Brubaker Colkins and Craig Tomashoff, "Oprah 1, Beef 0," *People Weekly*, March 16, 1998, 59.

77 CNN, "Oprah: 'Free Speech Rocks,'" *CNN*, February 26, 1998, http://www.cnn.com/us/9802/26/oprah.verdict/ (May 13, 2004).

78 Laura B. Randolph, "Oprah and Danny," *Ebony*, November 1998, 36.

79 Stodghill, 80.

79 Randolph, 36.

81 Johnson, 44.

81 Leslie Marshall and Dana Fineman, "The Intentional Oprah," *InStyle*, November 1998, 338.

83 Lynette Clemetson, "The Birth of a Network," *Newsweek*, November 15, 1999, 60.

85 Allen, 67.

85 Oprah Winfrey, *O: The Oprah Magazine*, September, 2000, n.p.

85 Mimi Avins, "Flocking to the Church of Oprah," *Los Angeles Times*, June 25, 2000.

87 Ibid.

87 Allen, 67.

88 Avins.

91 People, "Oprah Winfrey: Biography," *People*, 2008, http://www.people.com/people/oprah_winfrey/biography/0,,20006996_10,00.html (May 3, 2008).

93 Jed Dreben, "Oprah Winfrey: 'I Don't Regret' Opening School," *People*, December 12, 2007, http://www.people.com/people/article/0,,201657225,00.html (January 11, 2008).

94 Tim Nudd, "Oprah Winfrey & Barack Obama Hit the Campaign Trail," People, December 8, 2007, http://www.people.com/people/article/0,,20165011,00.html (M ay 3, 2008).

95 Ibid.

97 Powell, 112.

SELECTED BIBLIOGRAPHY

Allen, Jenny. "Oprah Winfrey." *US Weekly*, June 12, 2000.

Clemetson, Lynette. "The Birth of a Network." *Newsweek*, November 15, 1999.

Culhane, John. "Oprah Winfrey: How Truth Changed Her Life." *Reader's Digest*, February 1989.

Farley, Christopher John. "Queen of All Media." *Time*, October 5, 1998.

Good Housekeeping. "Girlfriends Are Forever." May 2000.

Greene, Bob, and Oprah Winfrey. *Make the Connection: Ten Steps to a Better Body—and a Better Life*. New York: Hyperion, 1999.

Grossberger, Lewis. "The Story of O." *MediaWeek*, April 24, 2000.

Johnson, Marilyn. "Oprah Winfrey." *Life*, September 1997.

King, Norman. *Everybody Loves Oprah*. New York: William Morrow and Co., 1987.

Malcolm, Shawna. "Oprah Mania." *Entertainment Weekly*, September 4, 1998.

"Oprah Winfrey." *Biography*, December 1998.

Oprah Winfrey: Heart of the Matter. VHS. ABC and A&E Networks, 1999.

Powell, Joanna. "Oprah's Awakening." *Good Housekeeping*, December 1998.

Randolph, Laura B. "Oprah Opens Up about Her Weight, Her Wedding and Why She Withheld the Book." *Ebony*, October 1993.

Russell, Lisa, and Cindy Dampier. "Oprah Winfrey." *People Weekly*, March 15, 1999.

Winfrey, Oprah, and Pearl Cleage. "The Courage to Dream!" *Essence*, December 1998.

FURTHER READING AND WEBSITES

Black History Month
http://www.galegroup.com/free_resources/bhm/
Read biographies of African Americans, including Oprah Winfrey, who have made a difference. You can also trace events that helped shape African American heritage and explore African American literature.

Blashfield, Jean F. *Oprah Winfrey*. New York: World Almanac, 2003.

Bloom, Harold, ed. *Toni Morrison's Beloved.* New York: Chelsea House Publications, 2004.

Cooper, Ilene. *Up Close: Oprah Winfrey*. New York: Puffin, 2008.

Cox, Vicki. *Maya Angelou.* New York: Chelsea House Publications, 2006.

Haskins, Jim. *Toni Morrison*. Minneapolis: Twenty-First Century Books, 2002.

Kite, L. Patricia. *Maya Angelou*. Minneapolis: Lerner Publications Company, 1998.

Lazo, Caroline. *Alice Walker: Freedom Writer*. Minneapolis: Lerner Publications Company, 2000.

National Women's Hall of Fame
http://www.greatwomen.org/
Biographies of famous women, including Oprah Winfrey, are featured on this website, along with a list of books about them.

Oprah.com
http://www.oprah.com/
Oprah Winfrey's home page includes links to her magazine, *O: The Oprah Magazine*; her TV show; a biography; book club; and more.

Oprah Winfrey
http://www.imdb.com/name/nm0001856/
Oprah Winfrey's film credits as a producer and actress, her other performances, and guest appearances are listed in this linked website.

Paprocki, Sherry Beck. *Oprah Winfrey: Talk Show Host and Media Magnate*. New York: Chelsea House Publications, 2006.

INDEX

PHOTO ACKNOWLEDGMENTS

The images in this book are used with the permission of: © Michelly Rall/Getty Images, pp. 1, 93 (bottom); © Michael Loccisano/FilmMagic/Getty Images, p. 3; © Buddy Mays/TRAVEL STOCK, p. 4; AP Photo, pp. 7, 12, 55, 64; Wisconsin Historical Society (52828), p. 10; © CBS Photo Archive/Hulton Archive/Getty Images, pp. 17, 18; Classmates Yearbooks, pp. 20, 24, 30; © Michael Ochs Archives/Getty Images, p. 26; ©Bettman/CORBIS, p. 29; © Roz Payne, p. 31; © Time Life Pictures/Getty Images, pp. 32, 47, 53; Hollywood Book and Poster, p. 34; Tennessee State University, p. 35; © Wikimedia Foundation , Inc., p. 38; Everett Collection, Inc., p. 41; © Ray Fisher/Time & Life Pictures/Getty Images, p. 43; © Kevin Horan/Time& Life Pictures/Getty Images, pp. 46, 52 99; © Frank Capri/Hulton Archive/Getty Images, p. 48; © Roger Karnbad/Michelson-Globe Photos, Inc., p. 49; © Ron Galella/Getty Images, p. 54; AP Photo/Charles Bennett, p. 58; © Jim Smeal/Getty Images, p. 59; © Michael Springer/Getty Images, p. 60; © Cynthia Johnson/Getty Images, pp. 62, 100; © Joseph Marzullo/Retna Ltd., p. 65; © Debra Lex/Time & Life Pictures /Getty Images, p. 66; AP Photo/Morry Gash, p. 70; © Don Emmert/Getty Images, p. 71; AP Photo/Michael Caulfield, p. 73; © Dave Allocca/Getty Images, p. 75; AP Photo/LM Okero, p. 76; © 2007 Getty Images, p. 78; © Ken Regan/ Time & Life Pictures/Getty Images, p. 79; © Marion Curtis/Time & Life Pictures/Getty Images, p. 81; © Evan Agostini/Getty Images, p. 82; © Per-Anders Pettersson/Getty Images, pp. 85, 93 (top); © Adriane Jaeckle/Getty Images, p. 88; © Jemal Countess/Getty Images, p. 90; AP Photo/The Chronicle, Carlos Antonio Rios, p. 91; AP Photo/Themba Hadebe, p. 92; © Scott Olson/Getty Images, p. 96 (top); © Independent Picture Service, p. 103.

Front Cover: © Jamie McCarthy/WireImage/Getty Images.

ABOUT THE AUTHOR

Katherine Krohn is the author of many books for young readers, including *Ella Fitzgerald: First Lady of Song*, *Rosie O'Donnell*, *Princess Diana*, *Shakira*, *Gwen Stefani*, and *Wild West Women*. Krohn is also a fiction writer and an artist. She lives with her family in Oregon.